SO YOU WANT
TO BE A
SOCIAL WORKER

Other Books in This Series

So You Want to Be a Social Worker

HELEN HARRIS PERLMAN

HARPER & ROW, PUBLISHERS
NEW YORK, EVANSTON, AND LONDON

CONTENTS

25/06

So You Want

To Be a

Social Worker

ONE

Who Are Social Workers?

AS SOON AS you think about a career in a profession, you wonder about the people in it: What are they like—these colleagues with whom you will be associated and actually live during all the hours of the working day? If you are thinking about entering social work, let me introduce you to three people who are typical social workers. Since you can best get an idea of what people are like when you see them in action (rather than when they only smile and say, "How nice to meet you!"), I'll put you behind a one-way screen where you can view them in the course of their typical day's activities.

Bill Shepard is a social group worker, who works in a neighborhood center. Sue Fairchild is a social caseworker, who works in a family service agency. Don Freeman is a community organizer, who works in a welfare council.

Bill Shepard: Group Worker

The place is a playroom in the Center. Sitting around the low table—or perhaps it would be more accurate to say

flopping, and wriggling about in their chairs—are about
ten little boys. They look the way all preadolescent boys look,
regardless of class or caste. That is to say, their faces are
slightly smudged with remains of an after school candy bar
or a hot dog's mustard, the hair on their heads rebels in all
directions or is so closely cropped as to allow wind and rain
to do the work of combs, their pullover shirts and corduroy
pants are skewed, too big when they're new, too small if
they're old. They are involved in the business of building
model boats—and the table is a clutter of paper plans and
balsa wood and jackknives and glue. But mostly they are
shouting and yelling about whether and how they will spend
their club money ("Jeez—we been paying *ten* cents a week
for years, seems like!") Is it to be a swimming party at the
"Y" pool or a weenie roast? The gist is something like
this:

"I say swimming party!"

"Yah—yah—a swimming party!"

"No, sir, you guys always have what you want. I want a
weenie roast!"

"*You*! You wanna weenie roast. Just too bad, you big fat
slob always wanting *eats*!" This is a sudden outburst from a
wiry pinch-faced boy whose face is livid with anger.

The other boys look startled. Slowly one of them points
at the attacker and then turns his forefinger in circular
motion at his temple. "That's what's the matter with Steve,"
he says meaningfully.

Steve sees this, doubles his fists, and suddenly, his thin face
pallid and his chin quivering, he crumples into his chair.

"You're yellow," a gentle-looking boy says mildly. But

Steve seems not to have heard him. He stares ahead with tear-blinded eyes.

Perhaps now for the first time you notice the husky young man who has been sitting at the table quietly working with several of the more boat concentrated boys while he listens and watches. He rises now, like a giant among Lilliputians, and with one motion goes to put a hand on Steve's shoulder.

"All right, fellows," says he, "let's get on with it. You were saying—"

There is obvious mutiny among the boys. They are silent. Several busy themselves elaborately with their boats; several sit eyeing one another and Steve and the young man who stands like a guardian at Steve's back.

"Listen, Mr. Shepard," one of the braver boys says, "that guy is nutsy." Steve sits motionless, staring straight ahead, but Bill Shepard, who has a hand on Steve's shoulder, can feel the light shivering in his thin body.

"Steve made a mistake," says Bill Shepard. "All of us make mistakes sometimes. Anybody here ever make a mistake?"

There is reluctant laughter and smiles of recognition among the boys. They are relieved that the tension is eased, and they are glad that a grownup understands that boys can do wrong things sometimes. "So let's get back to where we were," says Bill Shepard, resuming his seat, and in response the boys cheerfully pick up with their crude, bumbling eleven-year-old decision making process. All except Steve, who sits looking as if he had crawled inside a hole.

When the compromises have been worked over and the decisions arrived at ("the best thing yet, swimming and hot dogs after"), the group begins to take its happy, disorderly leave. "Bye!" "See you!" One says, "Thanks for helping with the boat, Mr. Shepard," and several others affably echo this amenity.

(They are unaware that the boats are simply one means to Bill Shepard's larger purpose—which in small part is to develop leisure-time interests and skills in young people, but in large part to develop in them the interest and skills in working and playing together with others, to begin early and repeatedly to practice at ways of working cooperatively with one's fellows.)

Steve is ignored by everyone—except Bill Shepard. "Stick around a minute, will you, Steve?" he asks, and then, as he notes the look of fright on the boy's face, he adds, "I need the help of a clean-up man."

Together, silently, they begin to clean the table of its scraps, and when Bill hands Steve a damp rag, the silent, cold-faced little boy scrubs the table-top with all his might.

"That's a good job you're doing, Steve," says Bill Shepard, appreciatively. "You're a good helper. But I'd like to talk to you about something else, too."

Steve's frightened eyes ask the question, "What?"

"I'd like to talk about your troubles with the other kids," says Bill.

"I got no troubles," Steve mutters, hanging his head.

"You've got troubles, all right, Steve. Lot's of 'em. Maybe you don't know it—but one of the things I'm here for is to help kids—help them have fun, and help them when they feel lousy inside, too."

You know by now that this pleasant, serious but easy

young man is a social group worker. Up to now Steve has seen him chiefly as a "nice man who plays with us kids." Matter of fact, coming from the family he does, having known only a harsh and drunken father as his idea of what a grown man is like, Steve has had a hard time making Bill Shepard out. He has yearned toward him; he has felt pangs of jealousy and even rage when he has seen Bill's warm smile and friendship given to other boys; he has felt good whenever Mr. Shepard has looked at him; but he has always expected that some day the blow would fall. "Is this it?" Steve wonders. "Is he gonna hit me? Kick me out?"

But Mr. Shepard is talking to him without anger in his face or tone, talking to him as if he felt for him—asking him what eats him, what hurts him—like a doctor, sort of . . .

Going through Bill Shepard's mind is the recognition that this troubled boy needs a lot more than group associations with other boys. He needs fathering, for one thing. He needs a chance to have a close, affectionate relationship with a protective, strong man whom he can trust, and look up to, and talk to. Maybe a man caseworker at the family agency. He needs understanding adults in his school environment and here at the Center, too, so that he can begin to trust the world about him. Maybe he needs a physical and psychiatric examination, too. But first, thinks Bill Shepard, I've got to get him to *want* to have some help, and then I'll call the family agency to see what we can work out together for Steve and his family. Something's got to happen fast for this kid before his disturbances get beyond control.

At the end of their brief talk (it must be brief because Bill has another group coming in a minute) Steve and Mr.

Shepard shake hands soberly. They have an agreement. They have agreed that Steve *is* unhappy, that he *does* have trouble with other kids, that maybe he *would* like to talk some more about it.

And here come the Terrible Tigers. At least that's what their red and black jackets proclaim them to be. They're big fellows, slickhaired, raucous, tough. Mostly they want to use the Center's basketball court. They're a group who were drawn into the Center by Bill Shephard during a period when he was working "on the street," getting to know and to be accepted by some of the delinquent or near-delinquent gangs that hung out at a near-by candy, cigarette, and (probably) bookie joint. After a few of the gang leaders had come to know and like Bill ("He's an all right guy—knows the score"), they took him up on his proposition that they and some of their cohorts come in and use the Center's resources. Then on the Center's basketball court they saw Bill able to outdribble, outshoot most of them ("Like real good, man," said one of the Tigers who fancies himself a beat), so his standing with the group went up a few more notches. One or two of them took him up, too, on the proposition that he'd be around if they wanted to talk anything over—maybe he could give them steers on jobs, or how to stay out of trouble, or . . . So now they come often, and occasionally they have a chewing-the-fat session with Bill before they go to the basketball court.

A few of the Tigers have been adjudged delinquents, involved in car thefts, are now on probation. Another few are drifters, boys who don't know what they want or what they're after, seemingly indifferent. But as Bill Shepard and any social worker would know, this is only a front to hide their anxiety about being unwanted and adrift. It's these one-time delinquents and these drifters that Bill Shepard and his agency, the Center, are particularly concerned about. If they can begin to feel they belong, that they are part of the community (the Center), are accepted by it, rather than being its outcasts and its enemies, if they can begin to feel some attachments of obligation and genuine liking for a community representative (which is what a social worker like Bill Shepard is), then they are less likely to act against the community's laws, more likely to want to be and to become persons that the community will accept and respect.

In the lead is Gary (his mother was a movie devotee). Gary is a hard one to stomach, even for a social worker. He's a needling, wheedling, sneering, sulky young man, an instigator of small, mean mischief. Bill Shepard is on the alert when he sees Gary leading—there's some nuisance brewing.

"Oh, Mr. Step-hard!" Gary sings out in falsetto. He has one hand on a swiveling hip. "Oh, Mr. Step-hard! We gotta invitation to a par-ty from some broads in here. The busy busty broads. They wannus to come to a par-ty—"

Bill knows what this is about. His co-worker Judy Keane has a group of adolescent girls, the Sociables, who have been casting eyes of late at several of the Terrible Tigers. And after much excited discussion they have decided to risk inviting them to a party. Bill and Judy have talked about it. They know it can become a ruckus or a frost unless it's planned and "handled" beforehand. So Bill picks up this opening.

"What are you telling me, Gary?" he asks quietly, ignoring Gary's posturings and the gang's snickers. "You saying you don't like broads? Or these broads? You don't want to go?"

Now a few of the boys turn on Gary, teasingly. "You afraid, Gare?" "Gare's afraid of girls!" Someone says, "Let's say we're coming and don't come." Someone else says, "Let's bring a coupla bottles along." They're scuffling and dancing about, each trying to outdo the other's ideas of how to make a mess of things.

Bill Shepard lays it on the line. Loudly, firmly, but without anger, he gives it to them straight. No liquor, no mean monkeyshines. Not at the Center. The Sociables have invited them because they want to meet some fellows they can be friends with. If you want that—swell. Come. If not, say, "No thanks." But that's the deal.

Gary is growling. "I'll say no thanks," and he hurls out an obscenity.

"Hell," says Tony, grinning at Bill. "I'll take a chance. What've I got to lose?"

There's a shifting and clustering of Tigers about Tony now. "Why not?" "Wotta we got to lose?" They shamble and bob and weave about Tony and Bill as they move onto the basketball floor. Bill blows the whistle for silence. "Listen —after the game—anyone who wants a lesson in how to act at a party, stick around."

Tony wants in—and several others follow him. Tony's a find, Bill Shepard thinks. He's a lively, quick-witted, imaginative boy with considerable leadership potential—for good or for bad. He has taken a liking to Bill Shepard—actually

Bill worked purposively to get this relationship—and of late he has come several times, privately, to talk over going back to high school, where to go to get the tests that will guide him to the right courses, how to connect up with a high school he dropped two years ago, what he wants to be and do. To his gang friends he has talked tough and boldly: "Listen, you wanna be a bum *all* your life? Not me, brother. I'm gonna make dough, see. Rich, see. Maybe I'll come around and give you a ride in my Cadillac . . ." To Bill Shepard he has talked more humbly: "I'll tell you, Mr. Shepard— kids like me grow up not knowing what they wanna be— or do—or what it's all about. First thing one day it seems like everyone's against you—at home they're always yelling, at school the teachers look at you like you're poison—so you think what the hell. But I see things different when I see someone—you know, straight—like you. I think maybe I could help kids like you do—if I ever got myself educated." Bill Shepard thinks maybe he could, too. He also thinks maybe the whole rumbling, unruly group of Tigers is worth cultivating and working with to bring this one bright, lost young man to fulfillment of his inborn potentials.

But Gary is hanging back, black-browed, sulking. Bill wonders if and how he or anyone else can ever reach this boy. Or is he an "untreatable"? These are questions social workers ask themselves many times in the course of their work.

Bill Shepard looks forward to supper at the center tonight. It'll only be hamburgers and coffee, rustled up in the small kitchen off the staff room, but Judy Keane will be there, because she's working tonight, too. Judy's a new ad-

dition to the Center staff, just recently graduated from a
school of social work. Bill's first impression of her was that
she was homely as a mud fence. But it turns out that she
has an infectious laugh and uncommon common sense, and
she's a wonderful listener when you need to blow off steam
(as when you've walked the tightrope with the Tigers, ac-
cepting them, yet holding them to limits). So Bill's begun to
think Judy has her points. (Wonder if she likes jazz?)

At seven-thirty the mothers begin to trundle in—actually
it's the Children and Coffee Club, as they have laughingly
named themselves. It began last year with a volunteer leader,
a group of neighborhood mothers who had come in for
some cooking and home economics lessons. This year they
have asked to bring some friends and to have "someone like
more of a teacher" for discussion of parent-child problems.
So Bill Shepard took it on. In the parlance of social work
it's now a group in "family life education." In the minds of
the group it's "a chance to have an evening out," to meet
some people, and "to learn, meanwhile, about what makes
kids the way they are."

Bill Shepard draws heavily on his knowledge of the dynamics of childhood to give them some understanding of what
makes children tick and of the interplay between parents
and children. He draws on his knowledge of parental problems and needs, too, and so he helps them to blow off steam,
to express their feelings of irritation and weariness and anxiety about Mary's temper tantrums, and Bobby's nail
biting, and Lola's sudden independence and insolence. He
uses, too, his understanding of group process (as he does in
every group he deals with), and acts not just as lecturer or

explainer but as one who draws from all members of the group the crumbs of wisdom and understanding they can bring to solving their own and one another's problems.

Discussion among the mothers continues after their more formal "meeting" into their coffee and cake time. They laugh a bit about their common problems, gain comfort in sighing together over how hard it is to raise children today: they need so much—it costs so much—you get so tired. Bill Shepard excuses himself now, and they bid him warm, reluctant goodbys.

"I think I'll call you *Dr.* Shepard," one of the women says shyly. "You're like a tonic for me."

In the quiet of his office at last, Bill draws on a cigarette and flips his calendar to look at the next day's work.

Sleep in the morning—thank heavens—he needs it.

"11 A.M. —Conf. Psych. Hosp. —Dr. L. and Marge Clement," the calendar says. This means driving out to a near-by hospital for the mentally ill where an experiment in group meetings among some of the patients is being tried. Margery Clement, also a social group worker, is responsible for this effort. The idea behind the experiment (being tried in many mental hospitals today) is to try to "socialize" patients, to draw them out from the isolation and inner brooding and separation from others that is both the effect and the cause of mental illness. It is to help these withdrawn, fearful men to begin to talk to others, to listen to others, and to find that they are not alone. They cannot do this by themselves—this, indeed, is the very nature of their sickness. They need the help, persistent, gentle, and supportive, of someone who can make clear what they mean, who can lead them across the bridge of empty silences between one another, who can talk over with them what to do today and what to look forward to tomorow. Because Margery Clement is a less experienced group worker than Bill Shepard she has arranged to use him as a once-a-month consultant, to discuss some of the problems she is encountering. Last month, for example, she had Bill sit by, as an observer, in her group of seven gray-faced, pajama-clad men. One of them talked as if he were wound up, excitedly, incessantly, overpowering the others. When Marge Clement suggested that someone else might want to say something, one of the others came in with some comments that were clearly on top of his mind but had nothing to do with what they had been talking about. The excited patient said, "You're nuts," and a third one said, "Who isn't?" and there had been faint general laughter across the group. Marge Clement's problems: To which do I have most responsibility—the group or an individual member of it? Then how do I check and balance those relationships? Tomorrow she and Bill Shepard and Dr. Leonard, one of the psychiatrists, will discuss this treatment problem further.

The calendar says: "1:30 call Fam. Agency re Steve." The caseworker there, Sue Fairchild, has been working with Steve White's mother for several months now (of that you'll learn more later). Bill Shepard wants to tell her some of his concerns about Steve, his obvious unhappiness, his alienation from the other boys.

"Call Voc. Ser. re Tony." (Tony is the Tiger, you remember, who thinks maybe he wants to go back and finish high school, but doesn't know for sure). Bill Shepard will arrange a date for some testing and vocational counseling—and, he thinks to himself, I'd better push to get it done fast—while Tony's motivation is still high!

"Conf. *c* A.H. and W.B. Clinic re: U.Ms. 3:00." This cryptic line means that Bill along with Allan Hart, the executive director, will meet with the head nurse and the social caseworker of the area's Well-Baby Clinic to confer about unmarried mothers. The problem is this: Among the many mothers who bring their babies to the Well-Baby Clinic for medical and psychological advice (a Department of Health service) are a scattering of young women whose babies have been born out of wedlock. "Young women" is really a euphemism. A number of these unmarried mothers are only girls who were in high school when their sexual misadventures left them pregnant. The consequences were the usual ones: shame, parental anger, expulsion from school, censure from their peers and neighbors, the disappearance usually of the once attentive boy friend—in short, a closing of all doors against them. There are many such unhappy young women in every city and town today, but the ones the Center will be concerned with tomorrow are those who are regularly bringing their babies to the clinic for care—those who want to do the best they can by these tiny human beings they've brought into the world, and who—perhaps—find the clinic one place they can go where they feel welcomed and accepted.

For some time the social caseworker in the Well-Baby Clinic along with the head nurse and several of the doctors have been aware of how narrow and frustrating the lives of these young mothers have become—no husbands, no love, no freedom, little money, few interests, little hope for the future.

Then one day the caseworker and one of the doctors together conceived the idea of some opportunity being offered these girls in the Center. Form a group for discussion of their common problems? Or for teaching them some child-care skills? For helping them pick up some high school subjects? For just "socializing"? Or for some combination of these? This is what Bill Shepard and the others will be putting their heads and plans together about tomorrow at the three o'clock meeting.

Finally the calendar says: "5:00—Conf. with jr. counselors." This will be Bill Shepard's regular weekly conference with three young people, aspiring group workers, who are leading small groups of youngsters in their recreational and getting-along-together activities, groups much like the one of which Steve is a member. With these junior counselors Bill Shepard discusses the programs they are planning, the purposes they are aiming to achieve, the problems they are encountering in the conduct of the groups or in the interactions among the children. He is helping them to understand and to deal with those problems. The junior counselors are volunteers, college students, selected for their skills as athletes or arts and crafts workers, but especially for their ability to interest and give leadership to children, and Bill Shepard is their teacher and supervisor. By the use of such volunteers the Center is able to offer many more activities and programs than it could otherwise do with its small professional staff.

Now Bill hears all the noise of groups leaving the Center—talk, laughter, the running feet of young ones, the slower pace of adults. He stamps out his cigarette and exhales a sigh of weariness along with blue-gray smoke. Heavy day, this was. Heavy day ahead, too. When he closes his office door behind him, Judy Keane is closing hers, too.

"I'm beat," says she.

"Me, too," says he. "How about some monotony for a change? Like pizza and coffee?"

Sue Fairchild: Caseworker

The scene: Family Service Agency—an organization set up to give help to people who are finding they can't cope with some problems in their everyday personal or family life. All you will see in the simple waiting room are chairs, magazines, a pleasant print or two on the walls. In one corner a little table and chairs and a shelf of toys and bright books attests to the fact that people often come here with little children. Beyond the waiting room are the offices of caseworkers—plain, uncluttered, allowing mostly for two or sometimes three people to talk to one another in quiet and privacy.

If you wait a bit, you will see Sue Fairchild and some of her colleagues come in. If you look at Sue carefully, you will see that she looks like hundreds of other young career women in their twenties—well put together, bright-eyed, pleasant-faced, freshly made up, good wool suit and smart pumps (though, to tell you the whole truth, there's a pair of flats in her bottom desk drawer for "beating the pavement").

It is about four years since Sue Fairchild was graduated from a school of social work. Following school she spent

her first three years as caseworker in a child welfare agency,
working mostly with cases of children whose parents were
unable or unfit because of their physical or, more often, their
emotional problems to give their children the care and guidance all children need. So the children had to be removed
from their own homes and placed with other families where
plenty of tender loving care and regular living habits could
be counted on to put security and reliability into their lives.
Like other caseworkers in that agency, Sue Fairchild had
had a three-sided task on almost every case: to help the new
foster parents to understand and nurture the personality
as well as the body of the child; to help the child himself
accept his separation from his own home and make all the
hard and bewildering adjustments to new parent-people,
new school, new friends, new ways of behaving; to help the
child's own parents (or one of them) regain sufficient possession of themselves so that some day they might regain
possession of the child.

This last year Sue had decided to come to work in the
family welfare agency to broaden her experience and, as she
put it, "to catch the family *before* it breaks up." Now, after
four years of practice, Sue Fairchild carries inside her sleek
brown head a wealth of knowledge about family life and marriage and parenthood and children and all the complex problems that people can get tied up in. Along with that knowledge she has deepened her understanding of human frailties
and foibles as well as her admiration for the strengths and
potentials that seems to lie in human beings side by side
with their weakness. Along with all this, Sue Fairchild has
developed many skilled ways by which to help people deal

with themselves and their problems. In short, it is a professionally knowing and competent caseworker you see in the pleasantly unassuming young woman walking in to begin her day's work.

She has no sooner gone into her office than her first client arrives—a well-dressed middle-aged woman whose handsome face is tight with tension. She is Mrs. Paul Silver, she tells the receptionist—nine o'clock appointment with Miss Fairchild—no, she has not been here before. Sitting across the room from her is a thin, gangling, melancholy-faced young Negro man, Mr. Amos Green. He will be seeing John Mann, one of Sue Fairchild's co-workers. Look at him, and you will be keenly aware of how troubled this young man is. His long fingers drum the chair arm nervously, his lips move, his eyes stare ahead. He will tell Mr. Mann his troubles in a few minutes. His wife disappeared three days ago. She'd been threatening to leave him ever since he lost his job. Now the children—two round-eyed little girls—keep asking him, "Where's Momma? Where's Momma?" A neighbor is feeding them, thank goodness. But for how long? And what is he to do? How will he get his wife back? And how can he look for a job now? You can see helplessness and worry written all over his young dark face.

But you may be wondering about why this well-put-together Mrs. Silver is here . . .

It's about her father, she tells Sue Fairchild when she's seated in her office. Terribly disturbing and embarrassing—she never dreamed she'd ever come to a social agency—matter of fact, she and her husband have been active contributors to social services for many years . . . But now, aided by Sue

Fairchild's warm sympathy, her attentiveness, her pertinent questions, her indications that she not only understands the problem but has ideas as to how it might be dealt with, Mrs. Silver pours out her story.

Yes, her father. He has lived with her and her husband and four children for the past ten years—since the death of her mother. He has always been a wonderful, gentle, intelligent man. But, in the last year or so—he's over eighty now—he has been breaking down. Not just physically, but mentally, too. He gets lost when he goes out—he leaves lighted cigarettes all over the house—he talks incessantly—he interferes in what she and her husband and the children do—he's childishly irritable and demanding. In short, he has begun to be a problem to everyone in the family, and she finds their whole life is becoming miserable because of him. She and her husband quarrel over what to do with him—and then are ashamed of themselves. Anne doesn't want to bring her friends home any more because Grandpa acts so odd—so there's another quarrel. Hugh was in a rage the other day because Grandpa messed up his whole stamp collection. Worst of all, she's constantly afraid for his safety and the family's—he might set his bed afire—the house afire. What to do? What to do?

Sue Fairchild knows the problem. The only "home for the aged" that might take Mrs. Silver's father is a cheerless place, overcrowded with physically and mentally deteriorated old people, poorly equipped to provide anything but bed and board. And Sue also knows, from what Mrs. Silver is telling her and from the quavering voice and hint of tears that accompany the story that even were there a better place, it would not be simple. The problem is not only: "Where shall I put him?" For Mrs. Silver, a loving, dutiful, conscience-heavy daughter, the problem also is: "*How* can I put him, my own father, out of my home?" How can she do so without feeling overwhelmed with guilt and shame? "What kind of example does that set for my own children?" And on and on, with examples of what the father's mental deterioration is doing to this family's well-being, alternating with expressions of guilt about her undaughterly feelings and anxiousness.

On the other side of the wall John Mann is hearing out the story of Amos Green and his unhappy marriage. Separated by the wall are these two human beings—separated even more firmly by lines of class, culture, color, educational background, and the particular kinds of life problem each is encountering now. Yet they are not so separate, after all, because both Mrs. Silver and Mr. Green are feeling the stress and conflicts and confusions that occur in the mind of each human being when he is caught up in some life problem that for reasons outside or inside himself he cannot seem to solve without help. Therefore on either side of the wall each caseworker is doing something of the same kind of thing. Each is hearing out his clients attentively, sensitive to nuances of their feelings as well as to their speech; helping them at times to express more clearly what they mean or how they feel and think; helping them to lay out and examine the facts of their problems; helping them to consider possible ways of going about finding some solutions.

For Mr. Green his caseworker is considering these measures: a housekeeper to care for the children, or their tempo-

rary placement in a foster home, while the father looks for
work and tries to trace his wife; financial assistance for food
and rent; equipping Mr. Green with some special skills so
he will not float from one job to another; a planned counseling program to bring about a better personality and matri-
monial adjustment between the young couple after Mrs.
Green has been located.

With Mrs. Silver, Sue Fairchild's plans are perhaps more
on the psychological side: to help this woman to express and
think about all her feelings of guilt and obligation and love,
and about her opposing feelings of anger and fear and fa-
tigue; to weigh these feelings (and those of her husband and
children) in order to be able to come to some decisions as to
what to do with this pathetic, broken old man who is her
father.

It may take a series of interviews to bring Mrs. Silver to
a resolution of her conflict, but after this one interview Sue
Fairchild will report to her supervisor "another case of in-
adequate resources for the care of the aged in this community." This family agency, along with other agencies in
the community, is collecting its day-to-day data on unmet
needs. These and like data are what get community social
workers (such as Don Freeman whom you will meet later)
to developing plans for the new or different kinds of resources needed to meet people's common problems.

When Mrs. Silver leaves ("I'll see you next week—and
many thanks again for your understanding!"), Sue Fairchild is on the phone, taking a call from Bill Shepard. It's
about Steve White. "Oh, yes," says Sue, "Steve's mother
is due in here any minute now. Let me call you back, Bill,

will you, after I've talked with her because I agree with you, we've got to work together on this one—but hard."

When Sue Fairchild ushers Mrs. White into her office, she is acutely aware of her pinched and bitter face. It's the same face Bill Shepard has seen on Steve. Is it a mean face? —or is it a hungry face, a face that shows love-hunger as well as food-hunger?

Mrs. White begins where she left off last week. "So Tuesday—or maybe it was Wednesday—he came home. Drunk again. So I said 'Where's your paycheck?' So he said . . ." It rolls out of Mrs. White, a smudgy repetitious story of her life with a man who has been a chronic alcoholic, a repeating deserter; a husband who has been brutal in his treatment when he is drunk, pathetically dependent on her attention when he is sober; a father who has viewed each child only as a competitor for his wife's attention and as another mouth to feed. Mrs. White (who married to escape from the misery of her poverty-stricken, fatherless home) has found herself continuously torn between pity and hate for her husband, pity and love and hopelessness about her children. Increasingly bitter about her fate, she has seen no way out of her problems.

Sue Fairchild is listening, responding with sympathetic understanding to Mrs. White's unhappiness, asking questions to clarify a point here and there, showing by every movement of her face and by everything she says that her intention and concern is to help Mrs. White in the best way she can. Clicking away in her mind are questions and ideas about what might and ought to be done. They run something like this: This is going to be a long, hard pull. This woman

is so discouraged, she has had so little in her life to give her
any basis for hope or confidence that I'm going to have to
work with her a long time before she's going to believe that
anyone really cares for her. Meantime I've got to pull in as
much help for her children as I can. Maybe that'll ease things
for Mrs. White, too. Maybe Bill Shepard can give Steve
more attention, maybe some fathering. An eleven-year-old
boy with a brutal father and a beat-down mother needs a man
to stand by him. Must see if I can get some day nursery care
for little Ronnie. It'll be good for him to be away from his
mother and good for her to have a few hours in the day for
herself. Yes, and either Bill Shepard or I have got to talk to
Steve's teacher. It's not clear whether Steve's dull or whether
he's so exhausted with worry that he just can't operate.
Maybe he needs some psychiatric help, too.

  Sue Fairchild thinks all this but doesn't barrage Mrs.
White with it all. She understands that the more burdened
a person feels, the less able he is to take in a lot of new ideas.
So she selects one, the one that may appeal to Mrs. White
most at first: the possibility of lifting some load from her
shoulders for part of the day by getting day nursery care
for Ronnie. Would Mrs. White be interested in that? Mrs.
White says, "Maybe." Sue Fairchild puts it another way.
It's good for a child, she suggests, especially when his mother
has worries and troubles, to be with other children his age
for part of the day. Mrs. White supposes that's right. Yes,
she guesses that would be a good thing for Ronnie. God knows
he doesn't have much fun hanging around *her* all day! So
that is settled. "And if we get Ronnie into a nursery," Sue
proposes, "maybe you can have a breather and think a bit

about Mamie White for a change?"

"Maybe," says Mamie White—and for the first time in the interview a smile—a reluctant, snaggle-toothed smile—creeps across her face.

"And then," says Sue, "maybe we can give you some help with Stevie, too. Mr. Shepard over at the Center tells me Stevie seems pretty sad these days."

"I feel sorry for that poor kid," says Mrs. White helplessly. (This is progress; for quite a time Mrs. White was able only to be sorry for herself). "He seems like mad or scared all the time. Sort of like I used to be when I was a kid."

"I'd guess you want better for him," Sue suggests, and Mrs. White's head bobs strongly in assent. And as Sue goes on to propose that she and Mr. Shepard will get together to see how they can help Steve, a faint smile of hopefulness lights up Mrs. White's drawn face.

When Mrs. White leaves, there are phone calls to make: to the nursery (Yes, they're expecting to have a vacancy in about three weeks—meantime if Miss Fairchild will get the child a physical examination); back to Bill Shepard at the Center ("Let's get together to talk over what to do about Steve and who will do it"). Later, says Sue to herself, I'll have to sit down and figure out how I can possibly get Mr. White to see me, to see whether there's anything I can do with him. Why, I wonder, does he so badly need alcohol as his escape? His unsatisfying work? Too much family too soon with too little maturity? . . . Much to be known and thought about here, says Sue to herself. But meantime she readies herself for her next client.

This promises to be pleasant. It is the last interview with

a young couple, Mr. and Mrs. Black. Four months ago they had come in agreeing on only one thing: Their marriage was on the rocks. Yes, they agreed on one other thing, too: Since they had two children—a three-year-old little girl and an eight-month-old baby boy—they thought they ought to "try to do something about it." They brought a pile-up of accusations and counteraccusations involving Mr. B's poor management of their neighborhood gift and book shop after Mrs. B withdrew to take care of home and babies, interferences from in-laws on both sides, Mrs. B's restiveness at being tied down to home and babies when she had always relished the sociability that being in the shop provided, Mr. B's withdrawal of affection as he found himself criticized and harangued by his wife and her sisters for what they considered his poor business judgment—a vicious circle of hurt feelings, self-protection, frustration, poor performance, hot anger, cool relationship.

These were basically intelligent young people, really motivated to make a fresh start with one another, though neither could untangle the network of anger and hurt in which they were enmeshed. Sue Fairchild was their untangler. In a series of discussions with them, sometimes with one, sometimes with both, she helped them sort out their feelings about themselves and one another, about what they wanted out of marriage, whether their expectations of each other were valid ones, about where their families came in and where, realistically, families ought to be kept out, about how anxiety or anger over something as mundane as paying the rent can affect how people feel and act toward one another sexually— and so on.

They worked at this, and over the weeks Mr. and Mrs. Black arrived at some greater understanding of themselves as individuals and as a twosome and, beyond that, as the foursome which, as parents, they had created. They made some changes in their situation, too—some provision for Mrs. B to be free to put in a few hours a week in the store (with agreements that Mr. B alone was to be "bookkeeper and boss"), and agreements that Miss Fairchild, not Mrs. B's sister, was to be her marriage counselor. Today they were coming in to take stock and to say they thought they could carry on by themselves.

When Sue walked into the waiting room to call them, she noted (with a rush of pleasure) the marked contrast between them today and that first day four months ago. Then each had sat tight, rigid, apart. Today their heads were together over a picture in some homemaker journal, and they were laughing together over whatever it was they saw.

"I'm sorry to leave you," says Mrs. Black, almost bashfully, when they leave, "but I'm glad we're a happy family again." Mr. Black nods and grins his agreement.

Right after lunch Sue's flat shoes come out of her bottom drawer, and her pumps go in, and she's off to the city hospital, several blocks away, where the psychiatric clinic is holding a staff meeting on one of her cases. Sue Fairchild and Dr. Jones, a psychiatrist, have been working together on this case. Dr. Jones's patient is fourteen-year-old Sammy Brown. Following the death of his father a year or so ago, Sammy began to have "heart attacks" and "weakness spells"— symptoms that his father had had prior to his death. But no physical basis could be found for these. Moreover, accom-

panying his physical symptoms were his loss of interest in
school and his unwillingness to let his mother out of his sight.
Sue's client is Sammy's mother—a gentle, whining, helpless
woman whose reaction to her husband's sickness was panic,
and to his death, endless mourning and clinging to her only
child, now babying him, now burdening him with her problems. Sammy has just had a complete checkup in the hospital. Now the psychiatrist who has been talking with him,
the psychologist who has given him some special tests, the
pediatrician who has done a complete physical examination
("no organic findings"), and Sue Fairchild, the social caseworker who has been working with Mrs. Brown about her
relationship to Sammy and about her own needs—all are
meeting together to pool their understanding of the psychological and social problems here, and to plan what can
be done by each of them to help this unhappy mother and
boy.

Sue Fairchild brings to this conference her understanding
and explanation of Mrs. Brown's own emotional sickness—
caused in part by her chronic anxiety and insecurity and in
part by her social isolation—no family, no friends, no interests outside her meticulous housekeeping. Sue has a number of ideas about treatment of these problems, too, and of
how to dovetail her part and that of the psychiatrist working
with Sammy. Her job will be Mrs. Brown, mostly, to offer
her in regular weekly interviews reassurance and support;
to show by interest and warmth and sympathy that there are
people who will stand by her in times of stress; to discuss
ways by which Mrs. Brown can fill in her life (possibly some

group at the center? P.T.A.? possibly some more solid tie-in with the church that she occasionally attends?) and ways by which a mother can release an adolescent boy to grow up, to feel his own strengths and lead his own life.

Dr. Jones agrees: He'll continue to work with Sammy's inner anxieties while Sue will work with those of Sammy's mother and also with the attitudes and actions of such other people who feed the boy's emotional sickness or can be helped to build his mental health. Among these, Sue suggests, are Sammy's teachers. They can make school a daily experience that is happy and absorbing or unpleasant and empty. So Sue will move forward on this at once.

Matter of fact, thinks Sue on her way back to her office, this might be a good case to bring to the teachers' discussion group for learning about how a child's emotional stress can create mental "blackouts" and physical "sickness." What Sue is thinking about here is the teachers' group she meets with every two weeks. This discussion group came into being after Sue and some of her caseworker colleagues had had a number of talks with teachers in this neighborhood school about children in their caseloads who were having one or another kind of trouble at home or in school. Several of the alert young teachers had grown interested in understanding more about how family life affects the personality growth and behavior of children, and the school principal and family agency director had agreed that one of the caseworkers would take on leadership of these discussions. Sue Fairchild volunteered and was accepted with pleasure by the teachers, with almost all of whom she had already worked. Now their bi-

monthly meetings burst with interest for all of them as Sue
or a teacher brings in some typical child problem, and they
discuss together its dynamics and its possible treatment.

Back at her office Sue is tired—"dead beat," says she,
stretching and grumbling a bit. It's not easy to be constantly
relating to other people, to be listening with all your antennae out, to be responding in terms of others' needs rather
than your own, to feel with people and yet to discipline yourself to remain balanced and objective. But this is part of the
gratification too, Sue Fairchild knows: that in the course of
any day a caseworker may vicariously lead many lives and
change the courses of some.

There's one more client to see before the day is over. But
the phone rings, and Sue takes just enough time to stretch
in her swivel chair and grin at the mouthpiece and say, "Hi,
darling. I'm fine. You, too? Let's have a quiet evening, shall
we? Like I'll cook you an omelet and you take me window-
shopping for a living room sofa? Good!" (That was Robert,
a young lawyer, soon to be her husband.) Sue is brighter-
eyed than before, but she switches off her personal life and
switches on her readiness for Barbara.

You can never really know what sixteen-year-old Barbara
will bring to her regular weekly interview. Sometimes she is
like an angry, small child, hating everyone—her parents,
teachers, even Miss Fairchild—fiercely. "I want to leave
home—I want to quit school—Why do I come in here to see
you, anyhow?"—on and on. Other times she's hardboiled,
wearing some boy's outsized black plastic jacket, slacks too
tight, eye makeup too thick. "After all, what do I care if my
parents think I'm a tramp. So I'm a tramp. And my teachers

—listen, Miss Fairchild—they're strictly from squaredom. I mean drips!"

"Then if you're such a big tramp," says Sue, working to keep her face straight, "why do you come in here to see me and talk to me?"

Barbara throws her a baleful look and crumples up a bit. Then tears, and the mascara begins to run, and she says, in a half-whisper, "*You* know! And *I* know. And who'm I kidding. I *want* to be different. I honestly do! I *think*."

Some weeks ago Barbara's parents, disgusted and despairing of this rebellious, hostile child, had brought her to the agency and simultaneously the school had called to speak of Barbara's high I.Q. and failing work. Reluctantly, suspiciously, Barbara had agreed to talk to a caseworker about what was bothering her. So she and Sue Fairchild have been at work, talking over and feeling through what Barbara wants for herself, how she wants to use the fine intelligence she has, what she wants to be as she grows into womanhood, what things her parents and her brothers do that bring out her rebellion and spite, what things *she* does that invite their punitive reprisals, how she *might* behave, and so on.

Here she comes now. Sue can tell by the way she's put together (hair brushed, just a touch of eye makeup) and by her cheerful "Hi!" that this has been a good week for Barbara. "I tried it!" she announces triumphantly even before she has seated herself. "I got that paper in. So Miss Storrs said, '*Well*, Barbara! This is *indeed* a surprise!' Sarcastic, sort of? So I was going to say something smart back, see, but I thought, Oh-oh—now what would Miss Fairchild say—So I smiled sweetly (here Barbara grimaces) and said, 'I'm *try-*

ing, Miss Storrs!' She looked at me, like shocked. Today we got the papers back. B plus! I practically fell dead. Wait'll my dad sees *that!*"

"That's good going, Barbara," says Sue Fairchild.

"Are you proud of me?" asks Barbara, challengingly, hopefully.

"I'm proud of you," says Sue. "But what's more important: Are *you* proud of you?"

They're off now—on the relation between the ways one acts and the ways others react and the ways one feels. My problem, Sue Fairchild thinks, is how to make this progress snowball. See Miss Storrs again; See Barbara's parents again! Get some recognition for her success! And—lots of patience and love and imagination and hope!

Don Freeman: Community Worker

It will be harder to see what this next social worker is doing. The reason is that so much of what Don Freeman does goes on behind the scenes. Don is a community worker— a social worker who finds out and studies a community's needs and problems and who then, working with many other people, organizes or develops the resources for meeting them. Let's look . . .

The scene is an ordinary meeting room, part of the Welfare Council's (or the Community Chest's) offices. A number of men and several women enter the room, singly or in pairs. The only way to describe them is to say they look like solid citizens, one and all. One compactly put-together, slightly graying man is doing the greeting and unobstrusively mak-

ing people comfortable: that's Don Freeman, the social
worker.

The meeting about to take place, arranged by him, is on
the problem of juvenile delinquency. In one particular part
of the town, the River Park area, there has in the past few
years been a bursting, wild growth of gang activities, petty
crimes, robberies, vandalism. Policing has been increased;
the juvenile court calendar is glutted with cases waiting to
be heard; but when they are heard, there is no adequate place
to put the delinquent boy or girl, except in overcrowded,
understaffed state reform schools which are schools in name
only. More truly they ought to be called prisons because they
simply enclose the youngster for a period of time. They do
not have the facilities nor has the legislature voted them the
funds by which education and rehabilitation of these young
offenders might take place. When the youngster is released,
he is less guilty than before about his crime or misdemeanor,
more likely to be hostile for the punishment he feels he has
received. He is more than likely to be returning to the same
family and the same circumstances that bred and promoted
his delinquent behavior in the first place. (This is another big
social problem, and at other levels than the one we're looking
at now, there will be social workers along with other professional, governmental, and lay people working on ways and
means to deal with this everpresent problem of how reform
schools can be developed that will truly "re-form" distorted
personalities, that will really educate—which is to say, that
will "lead out" the young delinquent from his antisocial to
socially constructive behavior.)

But let's get back to our committee. These particular men

and women have been gathered together by Don Freeman in this Welfare Council room today to see what can be done in a small way to prevent or at least diminish the incidence of delinquent behavior in the particular neighborhood of River Park. What can be done, they are asking themselves, to curb the contagion of juvenile crime?

A gray-haired man takes the chairman's seat, and after a short whispered conference with Don Freeman he calls the meeting to order and suggests that each person introduce himself. As we go around the table you will be less interested in their names than in what they represent and what they're like.

Mr. A—school principal of River Park High School—competent, understanding of kids and their problems, but increasingly harassed by truancy, vandalism on school property, "poisoning" of school morale by the "bad actors." Mr. A is eager to "get things going" on a community basis. Matter of fact, he was one of the persons who first brought the problem to the Welfare Council's (and Don Freeman's) attention.

Father B—parish priest, who is deeply concerned with the breakdown of young people's standards and morals and who has tried to deal with it among his own parishioners but who recognizes now that the problem takes more than one man and one church. He welcomed Don Freeman's invitation to come to this meeting.

Mrs. C—president of the P.T.A. in River Park's largest grade school—an aggressive, intelligent, active woman who is puzzled and angry about the problem, ready and eager to help with what's necessary.

Mr. D—manager of the River Park branch of the Citizen's Bank. He is a civic-minded man, committed to being a useful member of his community. He serves on the board of the Welfare Council and has agreed to chair this meeting, although he has expressed his doubts as to the value of it to Don Freeman.

Mrs. E—supervisor of the Family Service Association's River Park office (part of the same agency where Sue Fairchild is a caseworker)—a quiet, thoughtful middle-aged woman who returned to casework supervising when the last of her three children went off to college. Her agency has been dealing with a number of cases of school truancy and minor delinquency. She is ready to offer and to try to expand her agency's services to deal with individual problems of delinquency.

Miss F—secretary of the River Park Neighborhood Retail Store Association. This is a recently formed organization of small businesses in the area, banded together by concern about the changing population in the area, its deterioration, and the effect on business. Miss F is a bright, self-made, driving, vocal woman, herself the proprietor of the Kiddie Klothes shop. She has expressed in no uncertain terms her organization's determination to increase policing and arrests in the neighborhood, believes in "fighting fire with fire," thinks Don Freeman is "an idealist" (said in tones that imply that this is a synonym for being mentally defective), but "he's a nice fellow" and she'll come to this meeting "once anyhow."

Mr. G—representing the River Park Property Owners Association and also an officer in the local chapter of the American Legion. Mr. G has not committed himself one way or another in regard to this meeting. He is for protection of property; he is against "excessive demands" for property improvements. He is with Miss F in her stand on what ought to be done with "juveniles"; yet his Legion branch has indicated its interest in providing quarters and perhaps some money support for club rooms for boys. In short, Mr. G sits with a wary eye on Don Freeman, who encouraged him to come to this meeting, and on the other "do-gooders."

Mr. H—probation officer for the Family and Children's Court. Mr. H is a big, rough-hewn young Negro whose outward easiness and slangy speech often cover over the fact that he is an astute, knowledgeable, trained social worker whose special interest in delinquent youth has led him to choose this rugged job. Needless to say, he was one of the persons strongly behind this meeting.

Mr. I—executive director of the public assistance and child welfare agency that gives money, help, and various services to families and children. Many of the adolescents in trouble are from families in this agency's caseloads, and Mr. I, who is not a social worker but who has learned a lot about it from his staff, knows the many reasons why so many kids feel rebellious and hopeless and pitted against society. Sometimes he has thought, If we only had more caseworkers, other times, If we only had more adequate grants, other times, If people only wouldn't *have* children unless they are prepared to protect and love 'em! He looks forward to what possible solutions this meeting might bring.

Dr. J—psychiatrist, recently appointed to the new psychiatric service in the county hospital, a young doctor whose special interest has been in social psychiatry—that is, in those aspects of community life that impair or undermine mental health. Don Freeman has been eager to have him, along with the social workers present, share his understanding of the nature of delinquency: that it's something more complicated than "just plain mean kids from low-class families" (Miss F's explanation!).

Judge K—absent, Don Freeman reports. Judge K, now a lawyer in private practice, once sat on the Family Court bench. He is an older man whose record as jurist is one that has commanded respect from all persons in the community. He has considerable political influence, and for this reason Don Freeman worked long and hard to get his interest and support in this meeting. Judge K wasn't sure he had the time to give, wasn't sure this was the way to go at the problem, but was persuaded to come to this first meeting. Half an hour ago he called and said something had come up—and Don Freeman "understood" but promised also to call him further. (Mentally Don Freeman has made a note that he'll have to talk to Judge K again and work over whatever conflicts he has about tying in with the group.)

So here they are, ten people whose interest or concern about juvenile delinquency or about the problems of a neighborhood beset by delinquents, bring them together in this meeting room—ten very different people, from very different walks of life—and the eleventh, Mr. Don Freeman, social worker in community organization.

And what has Don Freeman had to do with each of them? And why? As a community worker his chief concerns are the social problems and unmet social needs of the whole or

any part of the community. As a professional in the Welfare
Council he is alert to problems that affect the lives of many
people, and his work is to solve or ameliorate them or, when
possible, to prevent them. Problems such as the rise of juvenile delinquency or the deterioration of neighborhoods or the
absence of resources don't just happen. People make them
happen. And they can't just be "fixed" by law or arrangements by some outside authority. People—the people whose
interests and powers and capacities to see that laws and arrangements hold and work out—must be involved. Don Freeman and other social workers know well that to gain the necessary acceptance, support, and active participation in working out solutions to such problems and preventing new ones,
individual members of a group must feel they have taken an
active part in the planning and had a voice in the final decisions.

This is why Don Freeman has been working for many
weeks just to get these ten people together. He has talked
to each of them separately, getting their particular slant on
what the problem is, what they think should be done about
it, what they would be willing to put into working on it, what
other persons with powers and interests and the means of
helping they think can be drawn in, and so on. You can imagine that with ten such different personalities and ten different motivations and several times ten ideas about the problem, Don Freeman would have had to plan his strategies
carefully and well! Today's meeting is the culmination of
these talks. Each of the people who has come is here not just
to sit back and to say in effect, "Okay—somebody—*do*
something!" Rather, through what has already gone on in

the one-to-one talks between him and Don Freeman, each is ready to put in his ideas and, Don Freeman hopes, to offer his backing plus the backing of the particular organization of people that almost everyone in this group has behind him.

It will not be a simple matter to get all these people to work together. People in the same community often have developed pleasant ways of greeting one another and agreeing that it's a wet spring or a hot summer, but when it comes to putting themselves into working together on a project that will take time and money and energy and heart, their prejudices and self-interests begin to show. For instance, Mr. G of the Property Owners Association is torn by whether he wants to help "juveniles" or clap them all in jail. Moreover, now that he finds a Negro at this meeting, he feels some uneasy stirrings of resistance in his breast. Mrs. C of the P.T.A. and Miss F of the Retail Store Association have in the past had some words with one another—when Mrs. C's son scratched Miss F's newly painted store front with his bike—and now they greet one another coolly and with obvious displeasure. Mr. A, school principal, wonders silently about the motives of Father B because he suspects that the parochial school attached to Father B's church manages to "kick out its bad kids" into his public school. And Judge K—perhaps the most important person for this meeting—has not even appeared.

To get these ten different people around the table together is only a first step. Now Don's real work begins—the work of helping the group keep before itself the fact that it has a common problem and common concerns; the work of helping each person in the group express his view of the situation

and his ideas of possible ways of coping with it; of encourag-
ing the more aggressive members to hold their fire a bit; of
helping the less aggressive to speak up; of trying to soothe
ruffled feathers, compromise differences, agree upon some
early steps. It is true that Mr. D, banker, is the group's
temporary chairman, representing the community's responsible, interested citizens. But without Don Freeman's coach-
ing as to who these various people are, what they represent,
how they feel and relate to one another—as well as to the
problem—Mr. D would be dealing with strangers in the
dark. Using Don Freeman's knowledge and experience and
anticipating that he can bank on Don's skill in drawing
people out and in getting them involved and cooperating
with one another, Mr. D finds himself beginning to think
that this *is* a good meeting. And that something may really
come of it!

Special skill is needed to help a number of individuals to
evolve into a cohesive group that begins to really work on a
problem, not just talk about it, to guide discussion so that
members consider all aspects and reach some agreements.
Don Freeman must use not only his knowledge of the particular social problem under discussion and the ways it might
be solved but also all his understanding of people and the
ways in which they can be influenced to cooperate. It is some
of this same knowledge and skill that Bill Shepard uses in
working with his Tigers or his boat-building eleven-year-
olds, or that Sue Fairchild uses in getting Barbara to work
with, rather than against, her teachers and parents, or in
getting Mrs. Brown to consider the possibilities of freeing
Sammy from her apronstrings.

As you watch, you will see that a number of suggestions are beginning to come out of the lively, even excited group discussion. Everybody agrees that something *must* be done. Everybody—or almost everybody—has a different idea of what. A recreation center or a boys' club is suggested. Mr. G thinks his Legion branch might be willing to raise money for this. Father B thinks the church basement might have the space; Mrs. C wonders if the P.T.A. might tie in here. Don Freeman moves in to approve and support all these ideas— they're good, something to consider further—but he reminds the group that lack of supervised recreation is not the root of delinquency. Dr. J, the psychiatrist, and the several other social workers pick up this idea. Recreation, yes, they say, but one must also attack causes. We need, they say, to do more to help these youngsters in their family relationships, in their school experiences.

Now Don Freeman asks how the social agencies and the schools might work more closely together to "tab" disruptive or disturbing youngsters, to offer casework services to them and their families, to develop special courses or tutoring (Mr. A, the principal, thinks this might be possible) for them when they begin to fail or lose interest in school. Better collaboration and mobilization of existing community resources could do much to attack the problem. But, Don suggets, more services are needed. Who will pay for the extra teachers needed? the extra caseworkers? the recreation workers? What special psychiatric and health and vocational and job-finding services might be necessary if an all-out attack on the problems of young outcasts is to take place?

Now it becomes clear that if they are to do more than a

patchwork job, they need the interest and support of the larger community. It is the chairman, Mr. D, who suggests that this is really a problem to bring to the mayor and the town council. The idea is picked up rapidly, and Don Freeman throws his support toward it strongly. Here's where Judge K, politically potent, might be of major service. Don suggests this. He suggests that the group decide which among them might best be part of a subcommittee with judge K to call on the mayor and other city officials to place the problem and needs and possible plans before them. Now, thinks Don Freeman, we're rolling . . . He knows, of course, that there will be many problems along the way, even within this planning group itself, that will require backtracking, replanning, clarifying, arbitrating, but the assemblage of people has become a working group, all interested in one aim—and this is all one can ask for a beginning.

Waiting patiently in his office for Don Freeman's return from this meeting are two pleasant-faced middle-aged women. They are the president and the secretary of the Norshore Philanthropic League. The N.P.L., an organization of well-to-do women who long ago banded together for reasons of sociability and then "to do some good," came to the Welfare Council a little more than a year ago to ask for guidance. What should they do with the money they raised every year through a money-making party they'd have "just for fun"? The leaders among them (Mrs. Dawson and Mrs. Burke waiting for Don now were most vocal) had begun to question the unplanned way in which they were scattering their money grants for this and that small charity and finally had proposed to their membership that they go to the Welfare Council for guidance.

Don Freeman was assigned as their consultant. As far as he was concerned they were the answer to a prayer. Because he had a project—a sort of happy fantasy—and suddenly, in the person of a pleasantly plump and intelligent Mrs. Burke and a lean, cheerful, and competent Mrs. Dawson, and all the plump, slim, intelligent, cheerful or dour, competent, and willing women they represented, he found the resources by which to make this fantasy come true.

It was this: For some years the social workers in the family agencies and in the recreation agencies, along with a few clergymen, had been reporting to the Welfare Council the increasing instances of old people who had neither the jobs, money, nor other means by which to occupy their time and their interests. A brief survey made by the research people on the Welfare Council staff showed that in one section of town—a neighborhood of rundown but respectable rooming houses—there was a large population of isolated aging men and women, each eking out a humble bread-and-margarine existence on pensions or relief or dwindling insurance monies, each living in a cheerless room or two in which they ate and slept—and then looked at the dingy wallpaper. True, on spring and summer days they could walk out a bit and find a bench on which to sun themselves. But for most of the year this was not possible—and, besides (as they said over and over again to the people who interviewed them), "You need someone to *talk* to sometimes, someone to *be* with, some place to *go* to, and something to *do* besides make your bed and wash your cup and saucer."

So, with the problem identified, Don Freeman had talked with his social worker colleagues, with the casework and group work representatives in this roominghouse area, with the interested churchmen. They had come up with the idea of developing a kind of daytime center or club in the neighborhood, specifically for old people. Here they could come for companionship, for talking together, for doing something with their hands and ears and eyes and minds, or for just sitting in a rocking chair in a cheerful airy room with other people nearby. They would, it was decided, have games—cards and checkers (or chess for the intellectuals), TV and recordplayers, shuffleboard and ring-toss (for the athletes), crafts and woodwork and instruction, perhaps organized discussion groups—whether about foreign policy or adult westerns it didn't really matter, as long as these lonely, isolated people found other people to talk and listen to.

Then someone suggested it might be nice to have a small kitchen-dining room part of such a center, so that there could be coffee time or even light lunches, so that people could eat together, because all of us, old people too, feel most sociable when joined together over food and drink. It was, in short, a fine idea, Don Freeman and his co-planners had thought, but where to find the money to rent quarters and furnish them— and—and—and . . . They had just about agreed on starting in a small way in one of the church basements when the N.P.L. came along, asking for guidance in how best to use its funds.

It was a solution—but, like most solutions to complex

problems, not easily arrived at. Some of the women in the N.P.L. were strongly set against the idea, didn't see the use of it; some disliked putting "all our eggs in one basket"; some had favorite charities of their own from which they did not want to withdraw the regular grant; and so forth. This meant that Don Freeman, as a community worker often must, took on the role of interpreter, speaker, consultant, and influencer. Even after the group had been won over and good quarters had been found, there were innumerable conflicts and problems, ranging from the ridiculous to the most important, from what colors the rooms should be painted to whether the executive should be a paid social worker or a committee of volunteers. Don was involved in many of these conflicts as well as in many of the forward-moving plans. He was, again, in his usual position of advising, consulting, helping to make connections and to ease communications among the many interested people involved, facilitating, enabling, supporting constructive ideas and efforts, raising "go slow" and "let's think it over" signs when questionable plans were afoot.

Now Mrs. Dawson and Mrs. Burke are here to drive Don Freeman over to take a look at the completed, about-to-be "opened for business" Senior Center. When Don has detached himself from the lingering last few members of the juvenile delinquency meeting, he hurries back to his office with pleasurable anticipation. He's at the beginning of one big job and at the end of another. It's gratifying and sustaining when it's an end that promises to have successful and happy results for many other people.

If you were to remain in Don Freeman's office while he's

gone and look into his files, you'd have some idea of the many
other community projects in which he's involved—in some in
a major, and in others a minor, way. Here's one folder tab-
bed "Foster Care—Mentally Ill." In this folder are minutes
of several meetings which tell of a project to develop homes
to which patients discharged from mental hospitals might
go. These are patients who cannot or ought not, for mental
health reasons, go back to their own families, or patients
who have no families at all. The world seems very complex
indeed to the lonely person who has been mentally sick. If
there could be found families who would take him in as a
family boarder, who would give him some warmth and interest and encouragement—his prospects for holding on to
recovery would be much increased. The idea was proposed
by the psychiatrists and the psychiatric caseworkers in the
state hospital for the mentally ill (remember the hospital
where Bill Shepard went to consult on group work?) The
problems are where and how to find the potential foster
families; how to interest people in offering their homes;
how to help people overcome their fears about "insanity";
where the hospital and its psychiatric caseworkers ought to
begin. They have sought consultation with the Welfare
Council on these problems, and Don Freeman, his fingers
on the pulse of the community and his eyes on its possibilities,
is there to help them plan their strategy.

Here's another folder: "Committee to Study Youth Employment." The problem: Increasing numbers of young
boys and girls leaving high school, either before they've finished or even after graduation, have no job skills to offer.
Jobs for the unskilled grow scarcer. More and more techni-

cally trained people are being sought. Schools do not provide such training yet. But even if they did, would it hold the youngsters who are having school trouble? Outcome: literally hordes of young people schoolless, jobless, goalless.

The problem of juvenile delinquency is closely tied in with this. (Some of Bill Shepard's Tigers are examples of such boys.) The problem of technological unemployment is part of it. (The sad-eyed young deserted husband and father waiting in Sue Fairchild's waiting room is an example of this.) The health of the whole community rests on having its members "at work" on something, aiming toward some goals. Therefore, the Welfare Council has organized a committee for the study of the problem and consequent planning. It is made up of businessmen, industrialists, labor representatives, and board of education personnel as well as several social work executives. Don Freeman is the coordinator and resource finder. He knows in advance that work with the committee itself will take considerable tact and skill. Tom King, head of the local branch of the meat-cutters union, and Jasper Hankins, president of a chain of food stores, have had some recent business altercations, and the fact that the eversmiling but iron-willed labor leader has won the countdown has not endeared him to his adversary. Don's task: how to get these two men to join hands and forces in the interest of a common problem.

The file of folders stretches back. Each holds the notes of community projects; some finished, some just begun, some halfway along; some successful, some failures; some frustrating, some heartbreaking; some gratifying—even elating. In all of them, in small or large part, Don Freeman has worked with, through, and for other people. He has worked with the aim of enabling them to build a better community, helping them to put their fingers on problems and needs. He has helped them collect data that will result both in their understanding of need and in their development of plans for action. And he has tried to influence people in their relationships with one another so that they will be more cooperative than competitive, less involved in themselves alone, more concerned with the interlockings between each man and the welfare of the whole community.

Sometimes at the end of a long, hard, wrangling or wangling day when Don Freeman goes home to his wife and children, he thinks, I dunno—maybe it would be better if you could prune and transplant people like rosebushes! But most days he goes back to the tiny community that is his family with the feeling that human beings and human problems are of never-ending interest and challenge.

Who are social workers? Here you've met three rather different people: two men, one rugged and boyish enough so that you'd look twice to differentiate him from some of the adolescents he's responsible for; one mature and steady enough so that you'd be unable to differentiate him from the other "solid citizens" to whom he gives leadership; one young woman, combining the freshness of youth with the poise of inner security. If you met them outside their jobs— at a party, for instance—you'd have a hard time placing them if they weren't talking shop. Their interests and talk might be largely about people, about local, national, and international problems, with more "inner space" than outer space concerns. On public issues they'd be likely to lean toward the liberal rather than the conservative side. They'd have quite different personal interests. Don is a gardener and camera hobbyist, president of his local P.T.A., a family man. Sue writes poetry in secret and paints with considerable flair for color and form, but recently she's put aside palette and brushes, a bit sadly, and has picked up cookbooks and pots in preparation for her soon-to-happen marriage. Bill is a good jazz pianist, a passable clarinetist, an ardent hockey fan, a fine basketball player, and a devourer of mystery paperbacks.

You've seen them in their different individual jobs. Yet they and their jobs are all contained within one profession, social work. What, exactly, is it?

TWO

What Is Social Work?

SOCIAL WORK IS simply a society's organized expression of concern for the physical and mental well-being of its members. It starts with a society's belief that people should have the right and the opportunity to lead personally satisfying and socially useful lives. It develops as a society takes stock of unmet human needs and of desirable human goals. This belief and this appraisal result in the invention, development, and organization of the means to provide for people's unmet needs or to enhance their social functioning. The organization of social provisions, social services, and helping processes is social work.

The moral principle that underlies social work is the belief that each man *is* his brother's keeper and that "no man is an island" unto himself. It is, moreover, accompanied by the democratic tenet that all men in our society have equal rights and that a society owes equality of opportunity to all its members.

From earliest times people have joined together to give some form of help to their less fortunate fellow men. In the ancient temple of Jerusalem, long before the birth of Christ, the Judaic community had organized a kind of relief for the poor: a room in the temple where those citizens with surplus crops or monies were expected to deposit their bounty unobtrusively and where the poor could come with equal anonymity to meet their needs. In medieval Europe monastic and other religious orders begged and distributed money for the poor. Sometimes, then as now, people gave money or goods or "helping hands" because it made them guilty or uncomfortable to see the suffering of others. Sometimes, then as now, they supported help to others because of some underlying fear that "there but for the grace of God go I." Sometimes they were motivated to give help and, even beyond that, to strive to prevent the causes of need, by their feelings of compassion, their awareness of the interrelatedness of one man and the other.

Today even a cynic, even the man who calls himself practical or hard-headed knows that in our complex and interlaced society what affects other men, as far away as Timbuctoo, affects him also sooner or later. One delinquent child in a schoolroom is a source of infection for other children. One bedraggled old woman searching in garbage cans for who knows what is a source of discomfort and uneasiness to all of us who pass her by. One family whose children show the scars of want or brutality is a festering sore on the body of the community.

So, out of many different personal motives, all of which had to do with man's relationship to man, and out of religious and social ideals that emphasized man's obligations to his fellow man, there developed certain organized aids to people who lacked the means to buy food and clothing and

shelter or carry out the ordinary activities of everyday life.
In this country (where social services are most fully developed) as late as last century these organized aids were chiefly
food and clothing handouts, sometimes money grants, sometimes—for some special occasion like Christmas or Thanks-
giving—a gift basket which held the cheerful glow of an
orange or the glint of a toy in addition to the drab staples
that flesh and bone required.

Old records in family service agencies early in the twentieth century carry entries like this: "Visited the H family,
all in bed to keep warm. Because of the bitter cold last week's
coal had been used up. Left $3 for coal." "Mr. G said he
had not been able to work this week because his horse died.
His family has been refused credit at the grocery. There is
no food or fuel in the house. He asks for $25 to buy a horse
so he can resume his peddling." You may be sure that in
those days that request would have had to come up for consideration by a board before it was granted. Twenty-five dol-
lars in cash was considered a sobering sum to entrust to a
poor man, even as late as the twentieth century.

But the board who would consider whether to buy Mr. G
a bony nag to pull his rickety wagon was already, mind you,
a group of people who were concerned not only with putting
one day's or one week's food into the hungry mouths of Mr.
G's children but, beyond this, with helping Mr. G to maintain his self-supporting activities. They were already interested not just in getting rid of Mr. G with a handout but in
preventing economic breakdown, in building up Mr. G's ini-
tiative as a breadwinner. In this sense they and the caseworkers were the forerunners of modern social work.

From earliest times in this country, too, another type of organized aid developed. This was the provision of shelters or institutions to care for men, women, and children with all manner of troubles and needs. Some of these were hospitals patterned after those in Europe, where the poor who were sick and disabled—young, old, men, women, children, physically sick, mentally sick, pregnant, dying—were clapped together to be given shelter and subsistence out of the way of the sturdy members of the community. (It took a long time before a hospital came to be thought of as a desirable place to go to when one was sick, and among some groups, for whom stories of those nineteenth-century hospitals were vivid, there still remains the idea that "a hospital is where you go to die"!) Other kinds of institution were orphanages where full orphans, part orphans, abandoned children, foundlings were all herded together. (Dickens' *Oliver Twist* gives a vivid picture of one of these dreary and dreadful places, and it served to alert many good people to conditions they scarcely knew of as they went about their own ordered and secure lives.) And there were the asylums and almshouses: the one where mentally sick and mentally deficient people were cast into wretched oblivion; the other where people who could not make a living were given a dirty corner to sleep in and a daily ration of bread.

All these were organizations set up for two purposes: to rid the community of its sick and poor and dependent and misfit people, so that these "lesser" human beings should not interfere with the welfare of its more fortunate citizens. The second purpose was to provide some means by which life, and then life with some decency, and then life with some open opportunity, might be sustained. Little by little these latter purposes became the primary ones of such organizations. Social reformers spearheaded this movement from the "handout" to the "buildup"; from viewing the poor and the sick as *les miserables* to seeing each person in the mass as a human being with human feelings and potentials; from providing meager shelter and food to providing a whole range of opportunities by which even the poor and the sick and the emotionally disturbed or otherwise handicapped human being could live in the community, go to school, work, have and hold a family, get medical care, find some recreation. These reformers made it their progressive mission to change social institutions so that they would truly meet human needs and enhance human life. Many of these reformers were clergymen, writers, physicians; others, not part of a profession then recognized, took the name "social workers."

The social workers of the nineteenth and early twentieth centuries were volunteers, men and women both. For some of them social work was a time filler, an avocational and "worthy" pursuit. Some of them were people with good hearts who wanted to be helpful to others. Some were people with grim consciences who wanted to reform others. Some, once they saw living conditions in slums or medical conditions in hospitals or working conditions in sweatshops, caught fire and burned with indignation at the social conditions that ground out the human-ness in men. From among all of these —the dabblers, the earnest, and the dedicated ones—there rose a small but staunch body of people who combined compassionate human feeling with sturdy social concerns, who had intellectual curiosity and vigor, and whose grasp of social problems and social needs was accompanied by vision about ways by which these needs might be met and problems prevented. Some of these men and women were giants: Arnold Toynbee, the uncle of the historian, Dorothea Dix, Samuel Gridley Howe, and Josephine Shaw Lowell are only a few among them. They and their like and all the hard-working but forgotten ones who fervently believed along with them that the welfare of each human being is the purpose and the test of a society—they were the forerunners and the shapers of modern social work.

You can imagine that if they came back today, they would scarcely believe the changes that have occurred in American society, in our social philosophy, in social work, and in social workers. They would be astounded to find that welfare is now big business. They would find that social welfare is considered everybody's business, of sufficient public concern for several major departments of the Federal Government to carry responsibility for it. They would find that many kinds of deteriorating sickness and permanent handicaps are being covered by great governmental insurance systems. Prevention of poverty and sickness is part of the program; and for such problems as have already occurred, state and town as well as the federal government offer financial help, medical care, and various forms of child welfare assistance. They would find a tremendous network of privately supported welfare agencies, too—family agencies, psychiatric clinics and hospitals, child guidance clinics, child care agencies—a bewildering range of ways and means to meet people's varied needs. If they struck up conversation with the proverbial man-in-the-street, they might find him wor-

ried that we were becoming a welfare state. They might be
naive enough to ask him what was wrong with that: Would
a "misery state" be preferable? And then they would find
that the word "welfare" had become loaded with all kinds
of emotions and misconceptions—but that in the last analysis
even this worrier about welfare believed in the right of the
individual to life with decency, liberty, and at least some
opportunity to pursue happiness.

Perhaps one of the things that would surprise the nineteenth-century social worker most (after he or she got over
his shock at all our new inventions and changed styles and
standards of living!) would be how our idea of human need
has changed. In his day it was assumed that the full stomach made a whole man. Today, for many reasons too complex
to be gone into here, we have become keenly aware that man
does not live by bread alone. Our ideas of what we want for
ourselves and for others, in terms of psychological and social
as well as physical well-being, have developed with all the
rapidity and intensity of other twentieth-century ideas. We
believe that a family needs not only a roof over its head and
food for its nurture but "good," "healthy" relationships
among its members. We have become concerned that marriages should hold and should be gratifying to husband and
wife, that children should be "understood" and helped to
unfold their full potentials of mind and personality, that
people should find their occupations and their relationships
with others rewarding and enhancing to their lives—and so
forth. So it is that the kinds of social service and the ways of
helping people have developed far beyond what pioneer
social workers would have dreamed of. And they would prob-

ably look with amazement both at the kinds of problems Bill
Shepard and Sue Fairchild and Don Freeman are dealing
with and at the knowledge and skill that they bring to those
problems.

Modern social work has become a profession. That means,
first of all, that it has marked off a particular area of human
living as its area of concern and expertness. Social welfare,
yours and mine, is the concern of a great number of professions. Education, medicine, engineering, the ministry, law
are all concerned with individual and societal welfare. Each
one concentrates on some particular aspect of human well-
being, and at points each may overlap with another profession, too. The profession of social work has points that overlap with medicine, psychiatry, law, education, recreational
work, and so on. But its particular and special concern is
with enabling people, singly or in groups, to work and
love and live together in ways that build their sense of human
dignity and social responsibility. The particular aim of
social work, then, is to restore, reinforce, or re-fashion ("reform" if you don't mind an out-of-style word) the efforts
people make to cope with their problems or to achieve their
goals in their functioning as social beings.

That's a big order. To bulwark this concern, commitment,
and aim, then, social work like other professions must have a
basic philosophy or guiding beliefs; a body of knowledge
about its area of concern and operation; certain skills and
processes by which it translates that knowledge into action;
and organized resources. Its practitioners—whether they be
group workers, caseworkers, community workers, researchers, administrators, they are social workers all—are selected

for their personal and intellectual ability to master the subject matter, to put their knowledge to use, and to identify with and be guided by the values and ethics of the profession. They are paid for their work, and they are committed to service and to advancement of the common good.

Does this sound ponderous and overwhelming? Perhaps some brief explanations and examples will give it life.

You may already have realized, as you watched Sue Fairchild, Bill Shepard, and Don Freeman, that they were working not just "by hunch and by golly" but by insights into the psychology of people they were dealing with. They were "tuned in" on what people were feeling and thinking, and this is what made them able to be helpful. Moreover, they had a grasp of what causes problems, what resources could be pulled in to deal with them, how needs differ from one person to another, and how treatment then needs to be differentiated. You may have noted the skill they used in the ways they related to people and how they tried to bring out the best potentials in each person whose lives they touched. These operations and the knowledge underlying them were studied and learned as part of their professional education.

You may have been aware, too, of how self-disciplined these three were. This is a major mark of a profession: that its practitioners are committed to using themselves in the service of others. A professional social worker must be aware and in control of his own needs and drives so that they don't get between him and the person he is trying to help. Of course this is not only a kind of ethical attitude, but it makes good common sense, too, because people are best empowered to work on their problems when their *own* motors are set running, not when they've been pushed or towed by the motor of someone else. Yet it is hard, this discipline and management of what *you* feel and what you'd like to have happen, when your client is being difficult (like Gary of the Terrible Tigers, or Barbara with her provocative "I dare you not to like me" attitudes, or Miss F of the River Park Retail Store Association) or unreasonable in the many ways people have of being unreasonable. Perhaps this is one of the main differences between the person who just happens into social work or even the dedicated volunteer of earlier days and today's professional social worker: that the professional has been trained to be self-aware and alert to the fact that it is not *his* feelings and drives that are to be gratified, but rather those of the person he is to help.

Along with other professions, social work has a basic code of ethics and a system of values which its practitioners profess. Among its most fundamental beliefs are these:

It affirms the sanctity of human life and therefore the dignity of every human being. By "dignity" we mean the inner push in every person to get up on his own two feet, to be seen and accepted by others as a creature of worth, as one who is like his fellow creatures and yet is his individual self also.

In their many different ways social workers try to uphold or reinforce the human dignity of people who are struggling against odds that sometimes demean them or lower their self-respect. They work to restore the sense of selfhood in people who have "given up"—an alcoholic, for instance, or the father of a family who throws up the sponge and deserts after months of unsuccessful job hunting. Acting on their belief in each man's worth, social workers attempt to bring about changes in society's appraisal of and attitudes toward certain outcast people—for example, to create understanding that the woman who has a baby out of wedlock is not necessarily evil or deserving of punishment. Social workers hold it to be true even of the person who seems to have become worthless to himself and his society, that as long as there is life in him there is also some flicker of aspiration to do or to be better than he is.

Another conviction in social work is the right of each person to self-determination, to be master of his own fate. This means that a person has the right to make his own choices as to what he will do and be. Practically, however, one's choices may be sharply limited by lack of means or opportunity. So social workers try to broaden the scope of opportunities for their clients. Practically, too, you can't freely choose what you will have or do or be unless you consider what the consequences of that decision will be for you and for others whose welfare is bound up with yours. So, much of the social worker's efforts go into helping individuals and groups to consider carefully the pros and cons of the actions they wish to take or avoid. The very process of this mulling over and thinking through, whether it occurs in one of Sue Fairchild's clients or in one of Don Freeman's committees, develops in people considered and thoughtful ways by which to make personal or communal decisions.

Self-determination is also limited by the rights of others. So social workers try to help people to achieve maximum freedom of choice and self-expression with the provisos that such choice will have constructive consequences and that such freedom does not infringe upon the rights and freedoms of other people. Sometimes social workers are caught in conflict as to where the rights of an individual leave off and his responsibilities to others or to the group take over. To help deal with this problem is another basic idea: that the person and his society are interdependent, that each takes from the other, each "owes" the other. Thus social workers formulate their aims in terms of helping people to lead personally satisfying *and* socially useful lives; and when they look at society at large, they say that the purpose and test of a good society is the welfare of the individual.

A profession offers its services not only through the knowledge and skills of its individual practitioners but through certain organized institutions which "bank" its wisdom, experience, and resources. Lawyers have a legal system and courts, doctors their hospitals and clinics and laboratories, teachers the school system, ministers the church. The laboratories and banked experience and organized resources and provisions of the profession of social work are social agencies (for more about them, see Chapter Four). Social workers are the representatives of social agencies or of social work departments of other welfare agencies. But social work—and therefore social workers—also carries the responsibility for building these agencies. In the first place it is concerned with identifying what social needs are unmet; then with studying what ways and means are necessary for meeting them; then with evaluating what present resources are available; then with helping to build new agencies or to develop or change the established ones so that social needs may be met more effectively and efficiently. Social work, then, is involved not only with finding and providing resources for people's social well-being but also with constantly studying, evaluating, and changing the resources and service and methods it has already developed. As such, the social work profession aims to be not merely a purveyor of social services but an instrument of social change.

But now I must call to your notice that while social work is a profession, it is a very young one. Compared to law or medicine or the ministry it is as yet in its early childhood. This is why in the minds of many people "social work" suggests some blurred image of "do-gooders" who combine hard-heartedness and soft-headedness, who are at once starry-eyed idealists (as if dull-eyed cynics were what this world needs!) and busybodies. Partly this confused image arises from people's confusion about whether they are willing to support and pay for the things they believe in. Partly it is due to people's generalizing from one encounter with one social worker who was not to their liking. Partly it is because many social work jobs—the ones most likely to be in public view, such as casework jobs in large public relief agencies—are held by people without professional training or by those who may not have identified themselves with social work or really be equipped to represent it.

This will probably be a problem in the development of social work as a profession for many years to come: that so many people who do social work have not been properly trained. Even if all the untrained social workers as of this moment were, by some magic, willing, able, and qualified to undertake professional education for social work, they could not do so. The fact is that today's schools of social work simply cannot take in or turn out the number of workers needed to man this country's major relief, family, and child welfare services. The prospect is that untrained social workers will for many years comprise the largest body of practitioners.

This would be a more serious obstacle to the development of the social work profession if it were not for this fact: The professional social worker is expected to undertake and to hold leadership positions. Opportunities for leadership as executives, supervisors, working-committee chairmen, demonstrators, and experimenters in social work practice are not only open to him; they are thrust upon him. The professional social worker is, or should be, social work's spokesman and representative. He is, or should be, his profession's severest critic and its molder. (This is one advantage of being a member of a young profession: it has few rigidities or sealed-off places; it is in a state of ferment and change.)

The oldest schools of social work, such as at the University of Chicago and the New York School of Social Work, are little more than fifty years old. It was only forty years ago that the first such school became part of a university (at the University of Chicago). Since then over sixty-three schools of social work have been established in universities in the United States and Canada. All of these offer professional education for social work. Some of them, in addition, are making outstanding contributions to social work's research and the development and organization of its knowledge—and from these scholarly efforts as well as from skilled practice the profession grows and gains stature.

Every professionally committed social worker belongs to the National Association of Social Workers. Only those with master's degrees in social work are now admitted to membership. The N.A.S.W. has over 150 chapters all over the United States (including Hawaii and Puerto Rico) and a membership of over 26,000 social workers. Through its chapters and national committees this organization of professionals deals with all kinds of problems: those that have to do with the social worker himself, such as his code of ethics and his agency's personnel practices and standards; and those that have to do with promoting social action and social change, such as producing a statement on public social policy and lobbying for or against legislation that bears on social welfare.

Because social work is a relatively young profession and because it deals with such a big and complicated area of human living, it takes a great deal of explaining, as you can see, to say what it is. It may be put into a nutshell by saying that social work is a profession devoted to restoring, reinforcing, and/or refashioning the social opportunities society offers its people, and to promoting the efforts people make to cope with their needs and problems. But once you have grasped that, you may wonder: So—what actually would I be doing if I were a social worker, in order to reinforce, refashion, and so on? This is what the next chapter will tell you.

THREE

What Does a Social Worker Do?

IN ORDER TO RESTORE, reinforce, or refashion the social functioning of individuals and groups, social workers must work for, with, and through people. There are no switches to pull or gadgets to push in social work. (Sometimes weary social workers wish there were!). There are only people.

There are the people who have problems and need help with them. There are the people who, by their actions or attitudes, make those problems better or worse. There are people who can provide help and people who, by their position and power, control circumstances that when bad create "social need" and when good constitute "social opportunity." Sometimes social workers talk of dealing with people and their environments, but when you take a good hard look at it, you'll see that, except for weather, natural objects, and the artifacts with which we surround ourselves, the environment that is important to us is made up of people—their actions, attitudes, and the organized operations they create and run. Our "social environment" is made up largely, of people, and social workers work with, for, and through these people, too.

Social workers help clients with all the kinds of social problem you can think of. They help parents with problems in relation to their children and children with problems in relation to their parents; they counsel husbands and wives who have marital conflicts; they place children in foster or adoptive homes when their parents cannot care for them; they help the patients of doctors and psychiatrists to find ways of managing their daily lives in spite of physical and emotional handicaps; they help adolescents and young adults find themselves and what they want to do with themselves. They help people in crises caused by loss of wages, by death, or by sudden illness, and they help people with problems in their social relationships which have been festering for many years.

In all of these problems and need situations (you saw examples in Sue Fairchild's office and in Bill Shepard's club rooms) social workers provide three things: social and psychological understanding; counseling and problem-solving help; and the practical aids, provisions, and resources in the form of people or materials, by which the problems can be met or at least modified. For example, take Mr. and Mrs. Black in Sue Fairchild's caseload, the couple with marital problems: they needed chiefly psychological understanding and casework counseling. Mrs. White, Steve's mother, needed these plus a great number of practical aids in order to deal with her problems: a nursery school to give care to her youngest child, the after-school play group (at the Center) where Steve could be helped to find courage to reach out to people, the psychiatric clinic to which Mr. White might be persuaded to go for his alcoholism. Moreover, Steve's "environment" in his school will have to be assessed and modified—which is to say that either Sue Fairchild or Bill Shepard will take the responsibility for talking to Steve's teachers and gaining their interest and cooperation in making school a likeable and liveable place for this troubled little boy.

Not only do social workers meet problems when and where they find them; increasingly, based on past experience, they are trying to prevent their happening at all. So they work at developing resources in anticipation of needs or toward prevention of difficulties. So Bill Shepard draws a mischief-making street gang into the partially controlled situation of the Center; he develops a mothers' discussion group to prepare mothers for meeting their children's growing-up difficulties. Sue Fairchild works with a group of teachers to prepare them to spot and deal understandingly with indications of trouble among the children in their classrooms. And, of course, Don Freeman has the development of the community's resources and open opportunities as his central concern.

So social workers deal with the people who have problems and with the people who need and want greater opportunities to stretch and expand their life experiences. And they also work with and through the people who, by their behavior and powers, have important effects upon those who are social work's primary clients. Bill Shepard and Sue Fairchild know, for example, that helping Steve to trust himself and others can happen only if the adults who are powerful in his life can be influenced to relate to him, consistently, in gentle, firm, unthreatening ways. So his mother will need help in this regard; hopefully, later, his father; right away, his teachers—and so on. Do you remember Margery Clement, the group worker in the psychiatric hospital who was using Bill Shepard as her consultant? Margery was helping a group of men in various stages of mental illness to talk and think together about real, everyday problems—to pull out of the unhappy dream world of psychosis. When these men are ready to leave the hospital and go back to their families, they are likely to find the same kind of stresses and difficulties that caused them to retire into fearful brooding in the first place. Unless—and this "unless" is important— their families and co-workers can be taught to respond to them differently, it is likely that their convalescence may be prolonged or jeopardized. Changes of this sort—in a wife's behavior and attitudes, in housing or boarding arrangements or whatever, can hardly take place without the help of another social worker in collaboration with Margery. That social worker, either a psychiatric caseworker on the hospital staff or a caseworker in a family agency, would deal with all the key people whose attitudes, actions, and resources have any bearing on the patient's welfare.

This is easier said than done. People do not change their behavior and attitudes toward others just because it's explained to them that they ought to or that it would be good for the other person if they did so. Mothers, teachers, landlords, friends, doctors—all of us—have our own feelings and desires, too, and it often takes a good deal of discussion and "working through" before these attitudes and motives are changed. Social workers do a great deal of their work, then, with and through the people around their clients who, by what they do and say, make the clients' lives better or worse.

In addition to the client's family and some of the other people he is associated with—employers, fellow workers, neighbors—there are many professional people whose actions may bear upon his welfare. Doctors, visiting nurses, courts with their judges, lawyers, or probation officers— these and other kinds of professional people are drawn by social workers into the orbit of planning for a client. The social worker's efforts with them is the coordination of what they are doing, the joint understanding of the person's or family's particular needs and particular feelings, and the joint agreements on how to help most effectively.

Last, there are those people who join together voluntarily, such as the members of a neighborhood association, or who are recruited by social workers, like those at the meeting in Don Freeman's office, for planning on some social problem or need. It might be a problem troubling people in the group themselves. For example, a neighborhood might be concerned about increasing vandalism, and people might join together and then seek a welfare council's guidance on how to cope with the problem. Or it might be a group of people called together to consider the needs and problems of other people in the community. Usually it is a combination of both. For example, the women of the Norshore Philanthropic League who, with Don Freeman's help, built a day center for old people: these women may be said to have had some need. It was to do something "worth while" with their time and resources. They needed a focus for those motivations. That focus was provided by information from and consultation with a social worker. A social problem was placed before them, and their interest was enlisted in helping to meet it.

You can see that, in tackling social problems social workers operate with, for, and through people. There is no other way by which a problem can be tackled. People must be alerted and interested; their motivations channeled; their doubts, questions, and resistances dealt with; their powers of intellect, money, interest, and influence measured and used.

People, people, people—of all ages, of all economic groups, of all nationalities and cultural groups, of all educational levels—this is the stuff social work is made of.

A caseworker like Sue Fairchild deals mostly with adults and children, either alone or as part of family groups, who are already under stress, already snowed under by their personal and situational problems. If the problems are not attended to, they may create widening rings of vicious circles. A group worker like Bill Shepard deals mostly with groups of children and adults who want or need association, informal education, or recreational experiences, and who, if the group were not available, would lack these opportunities. The community worker like Don Freeman deals mostly with people who want to tackle the already existing problems in some part of the community or to prevent the occurrence of new problems. These may be people who themselves are closely affected by the social problems they see and deplore, or people who reach beyond themselves as responsible citizens with obligations to help in community problem solving and resource development.

For all this variety of people two things hold true:

1. Some problem in their everyday living is undermining their peace of mind, creating distress or tension in them, destroying—or threatening to destroy—the conditions and relationships they consider desirable. This holds for the people in Sue Fairchild's office whose problems were purely personal, and it holds also for the people in Don Freeman's office who were concerned not primarily for their own welfare but for that of the whole community.

2. They have some wish or drive for better opportunities to gratify common human needs, to "re-create" themselves, to have companionship, to learn to relate to others in acceptable ways, to overcome fears of other people, to push back the too narrow borders of their lives. The people in Bill Shepard's groups, big and little, those in Sue Fairchild's office, and those who voluntarily group together for community projects all have these objectives, for themselves and/or for others.

So what does the social worker do?

You have already seen what social workers are trying to make happen in the lives of their clients and communities. For all the various projects and purposes they're involved in, and all the varieties of people they deal with, there are certain common "whats" and "hows" that characterize the professional social worker's methodology. These are social work's basic ways of doing:

1. *A social worker gets the facts about the problem.* People's problems have a way of sounding as if they were the same thing when they are simply called by familiar names—"delinquency", "marital discord", "poverty", "bad housing", "no recreational facilities," and so on. But the so-

cial worker knows that only one generalization can be made about problems. That is that every problem is different from every other one. It is different either in the elements that go to make it up or in the way it affects the particular people who have it. Therefore, a professional social worker doesn't conclude that one unmarried mother is just like another, or that bad housing is causing delinquency. Rather he gives himself over to finding out exactly what the particular facts of a particular situation are. What is *this* problem's nature? he asks himself. How and when did it come into being? Who and what is involved in creating it or in affecting its nature? Who and what is harmed by it? What importance does it have, as a social problem or for the particular people involved in it? This "getting the facts" holds across the board, from the caseworker who needs to learn from a mother when Tommy started to be truant and why, to the community worker who needs to find out what landlords are maintaining certain substandard housing.

Facts must be obtained not only about circumstances and activities but also about the human beings involved. Therefore:

2. *A social worker gets the facts about the people who are involved* in the problem either because they are hurt by it and/or because they are the potential problem solvers. Of course this doesn't mean that the social worker will need to know *all* about them. It means, rather, that he will want to understand certain things about people. His knowledge tells him that how people feel and think about their problems has a great deal to do with what they will be willing and able to do about them. It tells him that the best-laid plans and the

finest solutions will fall flat if the people for whom they are made have had no part in making them, or if they do not want them. It tells him that people mature and gain self-reliance as their potential capacities to think through a problem are drawn out and exercised; and that only as people are helped to express and deal with their distress and anxiousness and prejudices and angers will they be free enough to see straight and think clearly.

So the social worker works to ascertain and understand the person's feelings about the problem, the ways he is involved in it, his wishes and needs, his thinking about it and its solution, his willingness and capacity to grapple with it, what other people in his immediate life situation do to affect him, badly or well, and so forth.

In every branch of social work it is important to reach an understanding of (1) what the problem is; (2) the person or group with the problem; (3) the people who will be involved in working out a solution. Sue Fairchild needs to understand what makes Barbara feel and act as she does before she can help her effectively; Bill Shepard needs to understand what the Tigers want and why they act as they do before he can try to influence them; Don Freeman needs to draw out and give thought to the personalities and motives of everyone in his River Park planning group if he is to be successful in getting people to work together. But facts themselves are useless unless they add up to something. Therefore:

3. *The social worker sizes up these facts and their meanings.* He makes an assessment or diagnosis. He tries to put his finger on what seems to be the major need or trouble; what

seems to be causing it; how it affects and how it is affected by the people involved in it. Then he sizes up the potentials in the situation and in human and material resources for change or problem solving. What drives, abilities and aims, he asks himself, do I see in the people involved which might be mobilized and channeled for work on the problem? What can I or my agency or the community provide that would help meet the need?—and so forth.

This assessment or diagnosis is based on specific facts and viewed in the light of the social worker's knowledge and understanding of what these facts *mean*. This knowledge-based approach differentiates what a social worker does from what a well-intentioned and intelligent layman might do. The latter might jump from recognition of a problem to a prescription for its solution. The social worker goes beyond recognizing a problem to analyzing its special nature—the factors which brought it about and the most effective means of dealing with it in view of the social conditions and the human personalities involved. And then he asks himself: For this particular problem, involving this person or group with these feelings, aims, and capacities, what are the best ways of helping?

One of the ways of helping that is almost universal in social work is based on the proposition that man is helped best when his own powers are exercised. So:

4. *The social worker keeps his client working as an active participant* in clarifying the problem, his relationship to it, his assessment of it, and his wishes and ideas as to what to do about it. The reasons for this you already know.

But this is more easily said than done! Sometimes people

are so tired out or discouraged by their problems that they want someone else to take all responsibility for them. Some people—delinquents, for example—may not see their own need for help and are not sure anyhow that they can trust anyone with their innermost feelings. Some people want a ready-made solution in a neat package and are impatient with exploring the facts ("Don't bother me with the facts— I've got my mind made up!"). Each of these kinds of person calls for a different psychological approach by the social worker. But behind the differences of technique is the governing idea that what a person works out for himself is most likely to be acted on by him because it is *his*.

It would be simple, for example, for Sue Fairchild to say to Mrs. Brown, "Now, Mrs. Brown, Dr. Jones and I both think you ought to give Sammy more independence. He's a big boy now, you know . . .", etc., etc. Mrs. Brown would probably say, "Yes, yes," and go her own way. Sue Fairchild —and any other professional social caseworker—would rather say something like, "Mrs. Brown, I know you've done a lot of thinking, and worrying, too, about what Sammy ought to be like. Tell me, what would you want for him? to be? to do?" Later—much later—"How do you suppose Sammy can get to be the man you want him to be? Do you suppose you could take the gamble of letting him, say, stay with some of the other boys after school? join a club maybe? come home when you're not there and let himself in, and fix his own snack?" It's a long process sometimes, the process of involving another person's thinking and feeling, of getting him to take new actions in his own behalf—but it's the process that helps people better to become their own problem solvers.

This same process of involving the client as participant
and actor occurs throughout social work. You can see how
Don Freeman would be working this way, too, in his community operations.

But, you may ask, how does the social worker get people
to want to take the trouble to change their behavior or their
problem or the way they go about dealing with their problem?

5. *The social worker offers his clients a sustaining relationship* characterized by warmth of feeling and steadiness
of acceptance.

People who are under stress of problems or troubles or
people who are reaching out for new experiences feel released and empowered when another person who seems steady
and trustworthy indicates that he's with them. All of us gain
inner strength and security from good relationships with
people we respect and trust. Not all of us have such people
standing by when we most need them. Social workers know
the importance of borrowing strength from another, of feeling surer because a person who is likeable shows that he
likes you. They know that the emotional linkage of good relationships can nourish and sustain people through crises
and over long stretches of difficulty.

Therefore, from the very first day of his training, the
social worker is kept aware of the importance of warmth and
acceptance in promoting human growth, of being "client-
centered" and managing to control his own subjectivities, of
using himself in such ways as to say in effect, "I am *with*
you and I am *for* you. I am *with* you in my acceptance of
your feelings. I am *for* you to help you find some better way

to be or act or work out your problem."

It is easy to see how strong supportive relationships would be basic to the help Sue Fairchild would be giving to a Mrs. Silver or a Mrs. Brown or a Barbara. It is clear that Bill Shepard would have to work hard to establish strong, friendly, yet controlled relationships with his groups. Even Don Freeman whose clients are often "powers" in the community must forget his own biases and personal feelings and lend himself to the needs of the group members with steadiness, acceptance, and objectivity so they will feel understood and supported in their various efforts and the work can be carried forward with singleness of purpose.

6. Within this sustaining relationship, *the social worker helps his client to recognize and express the feelings that hamper him* or stand in the way of his adequate functioning. When people have difficult problems, they are often so full of anxiety or guilt or white-hot anger, or black cold despair that they cannot do anything but try to keep the lid on their emotions. Their feelings paralyze them or rise like clouds before their eyes and keep them from seeing straight or clearly. Then their actions in relation to their problems are likely to be poorly planned or even inappropriate. Social workers understand all this and therefore they always attend to what and how people are feeling. They help people to speak out, to express their emotions, and by their acceptance and talking these feelings over (sometimes over and over and over again!) they help to dilute or even radically change them, and thus change the person's slant on his problem and his behavior.

This happens all the time in casework: that caseworkers

need to help people know and work over the emotions that crowd in on them and complicate their problems. It often happens in group work—when the feelings and consequent behavior of one member of a group skews the group's activities and relationships, as when Steve exploded in the boat-building group. Then the group worker knows he has to pay particular attention or give particular help to the one or several persons who are emotionally disturbed and disturbing. And it is not a bit unusual for people who are working with a community worker, ostensibly to give service to others, to become quite emotionally upset and involved. The social worker does not in any sense begin to "treat" them; but he will surely have to find out from them what's behind their grim determination to do this or that, their violent prejudice about him or her, their opposition to one or another plan. For instance, when Don Freeman persuaded Miss F to come to the meeting on juvenile delinquency, he was successful only because he first gave Miss F full opportunity to have her emotional say about all the terrible people moving into this neighborhood. He didn't agree with her, mind you, and he made that clear. He also made clear, however, that he could surely appreciate her position for *her*—and that's why he wanted her to take part in planning what to do.

With a relationship of trust and acceptance established,

7. *The social worker supports and exercises his client's own powers of thought and action.* This means that along with talking over "how I feel," the client is stimulated to consider, together with the social worker, "how I think about these feelings, how I think about my behavior, my problems, and the reasons for them." And then, from there: What can I do,

by myself or with others, to create a better situation? And
then, What do I want to do differently, and how do I want
to be different? All these questions and all the possible alternatives are talked over and over between the social worker
and his client, with the social worker always asking questions
and making comments which will stimulate the client to understand and handle his feelings and to use the best powers
of will, thought, and resources he can muster to find his own
answers. Of course, those "best powers" may fall short, so
the social worker contributes such knowledge or ideas as he
may have for the client's consideration. Sometimes he takes
such action or provides such means as the client does not
have or cannot take alone.

In brief, the social worker helps his client continuously to
weave to and fro between his feelings, his thinking, his resources, and his goals. With people who are fairly well balanced and whose problems are not too stressful, this weaving
together from problem recognition to problem solving is very
quickly done. It did not take too long, for example, for the
discussions to take place in the Norshore Philanthropic
League which culminated in the decision to put all its energy
and money into the project Don Freeman proposed. But
when people are deeply troubled, when they are "*in* trouble,"
and their social situation is not very supportive, it takes a
social worker (usually a caseworker) many months of re-
peated talking together, feeling through, thinking through,
trying out, before his client feels ready to try his own wings.

To try his own wings requires increased inner security and
stability. But in many cases it also requires that there be
tangible resources outside the person too. This means that

8. *The social worker must plan for, mobilize, and develop such opportunities and material means as are necessary for the solution of his client's problem; and show him how to avail himself of these resources.* Man cannot live by bread alone, it is true. But he cannot live by guidance and counseling alone either.

A group worker like Bill Shepard would find his scope of opportunity provision very narrow indeed if he did not have materials with which children could work, a gym where boys could discharge physical energies in socially approved and safe ways, a family agency to which he could turn with a child's problems, a kitchen where girls could cook up a party. A caseworker like Sue Fairchild would be very limited in her ability to be helpful if it were not for the cooperating psychiatric clinic for a Sammy Brown, the Center or the home for aged people for a Mrs. Silver's father, the homemaker service developed by the agency to provide a temporary mother substitute for Mr. Green's little girls until their mother came back, and so on. And, of course, without the manpower and work hours and money proffered by community people, a Don Freeman could not begin to carry into action his well-laid plans for social services.

The good social worker knows the organized resources in his community. He knows how essential they are to fill the lacks in people's lives. He may have to work for some time to get his particular client to want to use them. Sometimes he may have to bring the mountain to Mohammed, and sometimes he may have to work with the resource (as Don Freeman did with the N.P.L.) to get it to shape itself to the needs of a person or of the community. But he never loses sight of the fact that people live in relation to other people and to social conditions and institutions. The social worker is a bridging person, a linker between individuals and groups and the various opportunities and helps that our society has set up.

Beyond this, the good social worker keeps his eyes and ears open to what services in his community are lacking, what unmet needs there are for which no resources exist, what kinds of concrete "helps" need to be developed. Caseworkers, particularly, are the advance-scout people in this part of social work. Caseworkers deal with people in trouble. They know first-hand how frequently certain problems occur and what the needs seem to be. Their reports to supervisory and administrative personnel in their agencies about what people seem to be hurt by and to be wanting becomes the basis of planning by one or more agencies for change or new developments in the social services.

There is one further aspect of every social worker's job. That is taking social action. Social action actually embraces everything you have already seen social workers doing with and for people, But it involves action at a more general level, too, action that has to do with legislative and judicial matters. Good social workers keep abreast of court and political actions and of social trends, keep an eye on how this housing bill or that school or court ruling affects the welfare of people, particularly of those people who often lack a spokesman. Their experience as practitioners equips them to know a great deal directly about how policies and laws affect the everyday life of men, women, and children. Through their professional organization, the National Association of Social

Workers, social workers serve on committees to study local or federal legislation and policy proposals and to develop plans that promote or protest, as the case may be, the proposed action. With their agencies—their boards of directors and executives—they may take a united stand on needed reforms in courts, jails, mental hospitals, children's institutions, and so forth. Of course, as a private citizen the social worker thinks and speaks out and acts on the basis of his first-hand professional knowledge both of human need and of the effect of legal and social actions and establishments upon the common good.

The professional social worker, then, is a social actionist sometimes only within the boundaries of his own job but often outside those boundaries, too, joined by his fellow social workers and other professional and lay people in working on some immediate or long-range cause.

When you saw Sue and Bill and Don at their work, you saw them alone with their clients, individuals or groups, housed in a certain kind of social agency. Social agencies are organizations of certain functions and services. They are "where social workers work," but they are more than that, too. *Where* social workers work has a good deal to do with exactly *what* they do. The next chapter will tell you about this.

FOUR

Where Do Social Workers Work?

WHAT A SOCIAL WORKER does depends in many ways on where he works. "Where" is some kind of social agency. If you were to become a social worker, where you would work would depend first on what kind of social work you decided you wanted to do: whether you chose to be a caseworker, a group worker, or a community worker. Once you had made that choice, you'd have further choice ahead of you. Geographically your "where" could be almost anywhere in the country. But more important would be what sort of social problem you were interested in working with. Social agencies are set up to deal with various aspects of people's social needs. Where you would work would depend on your particular interest and choice as well as your particular capacities and training.

As you read what follows, remember this: Once you have mastered one of the major methods in social work—which is to say, once you have become a caseworker, a group worker, or a community worker—it is possible for you to work in many different social agencies or social work departments that use your particular method. For example, once you have become a caseworker, you may work for several years in a family service agency, you may move to a psychiatric clinic, you may move from there (not too frequent moves, hopefully!) to a child-treatment institution, and so forth. Once you have become a group worker, you may work in a settlement house, you may take your next job in a psychiatric hospital, and so forth. Social workers are a mobile group—partly because so many new opportunities are opening up to them. But wherever they go they are employees of social agencies or social work departments (except for a small sector of social workers who are private practitioners and who will be discussed at this chapter's end), and therefore they, and you, will need to understand what social agencies are.

Social work is practiced in social agencies or in departments of social service that are a part of other human welfare organizations, such as schools, hospitals, courts, etc. A social agency (let's use that term to cover both sorts of setting) is simply the formal organization of resources—money, services, and manpower—to meet certain kinds of social problem and to provide for certain social needs. It comes into being when citizens of a local community or of a nation recognize that social needs exist for which dependable, organized, expert resources are necessary. So an agency is created to perform special functions, to give help or offer opportunities. It may be supported by taxes, as are public assistance agencies, veterans' hospitals and clinics, community mental health clinics, court probation departments, etc. Or it may be supported by voluntary contributions, as are many of the family and child welfare agencies and clinics that you are accustomed to thinking of as "Red Feather," or Community Chest, agencies.

Every social agency must have a permit or a charter from official sources that says it meets certain standards. Every agency has a board of directors, or some similar governing body, that carries over-all responsibilities for the agency's activities. Every agency has rules and regulations that say what its program is, who is eligible for its services, how it aims to give those services. Its administrative and supervisory personnel—social workers—are accountable for its effective and efficient operation; and its practitioners—the social workers who actually *are* the agency in action—are you and your colleagues. You have the direct contact with the people who look to the agency for the kinds of knowledge and services it holds and transmits through you.

If and when you become a social worker, here are the kinds of place where you could be employed:

Family Welfare Agencies

The family is the basic and most vital social unit in our society. So it is no wonder that the family welfare agency was one of the first kinds of social service agency to be developed, and that it remains the most central agency in the galaxy of social services.

A family's welfare depends first and foremost on having its food and shelter and basic clothing needs met. So the basic family welfare agencies are the tax-supported *public assistance agencies* which provide "relief," or money grants to families (and individuals without families) for their basic health and decency needs. There are many reasons why people

need relief. There are families of mothers and their children
where the natural breadwinner, the father, is physically or
mentally sick—sometimes temporarily, sometimes forever;
where the father has died or has deserted; where there never
was a father—that is, where the children are the pathetic result of sex relations outside of marriage; where the man who
is father and husband has never adequately carried his responsibility; where the father has a job and works as hard as
he can, but because he has no special skills or occupational
preparation, he is the last to be hired, the first to be fired,
and even when he has work, earns too little to put milk in
the children's stomachs and shoes on their feet.

Even if you go no further than this in thinking about
families on relief, you can see why there must be dependable
organized means to provide money assistance. Perhaps you
can also see why social workers rather than just money-
handout machines are vitally necessary. It is because people
—men, women, and children—are all involved in these problems that make relief necessary. They are not just bodies,
not just statistics. They *feel* these needs. Not only their
stomachs are involved but also their sense of hope or despair,
of being worthless or worth while, of being outcasts or accepted. Moreover, their problems are all different from one
another. The family whose father lies bedridden has many
very different problems from the family where there never
was a father, and both are very different from the family
where the husband and father is up against continuous unemployment. All of these families, to be sure, have the problem of no money, but the reason for no money is different

for each of them, as are the family strengths and difficulties and the possible solutions.

It is unfortunate that to this date most of the caseworkers in the public aid agencies are untrained people who do not have the knowledge to truly understand personal and family problems or the skills to strengthen family life. (There are simply not enough trained caseworkers to go around.) Moreover, these untrained caseworkers are overloaded with too many cases and tasks. But within these agencies there are responsible and continuous efforts to give on-the-job training and encourage caseworkers to take time off to go to a school of social work. It is clearly recognized that relief grants will be needed for many familes until key members have been rehabilitated physically and/or psychologically; and trained social workers are better equipped to speed this process.

Family welfare begins with firm floor-boards of economic security under a family's feet. But economic security does not guarantee personal and interpersonal contentment. Family troubles occur in every segment of society, among the rich as well as the poor. Quarrels and incompatibility between husbands and wives affect not only their own mental health but that of their children, too. Marital problems quickly give rise to parent-child problems, child-school problems, and husband-employment problems. The chain reaction may run in reverse, too: A child with physical or emotional problems may set off a whole chain of disruptions in the family life, affecting sisters and brothers, parents, neighboring children, and so on.

It was when communities recognized and became concerned about the emotional well-being of families as well as their economic welfare that *family service agencies* spread across the country. Today there are well over three hundred family service agencies in this country, supported by voluntary contributions (through Community Chests and federated funds), to provide casework help to husbands and wives, parents and young children, adult children and aged parents, who are caught up in conflicts that shake family or individual stability. These agencies hire only professionally trained social workers because the problems with which they deal require all the social and psychological knowledge the social work profession has—and then some!

The voluntarily supported, so-called "private" family welfare agency today has another major function. Not only does it deal with all the emotional-social problems that rock family life and undermine the social functioning and personality development of its members; it is, in addition, an experimental laboratory where new approaches to family problems are being tried out. Recently, for example, family agencies have been experimenting with "family life education," where mothers and fathers meet in group sessions to learn more about child-rearing and to anticipate and thus avoid problems.

Sometimes family life is already so torn to pieces, so sick, or so fragile by the time it comes to the attention of social workers that the children of the family are in danger of being—or already have been—seriously harmed. This harm to children may be actually physical, the result of brutal treatment or consistent neglect. Or the harm may be psycho-

logical. This almost always accompanies physical depriva-
tion or hurt but may occur when the child is clean and well
fed, too. For example, it occurs when the parent is indifferent, totally absorbed in himself and his own problems, when
the parent is rejecting and harsh, or when, as is so often the
case, the parent himself is only a child in an adult body, lacking the mental and emotional ability to be a real parent.

Child Welfare Agencies

It was to protect the physical and personality development
of children that child welfare agencies came into being. These
are of many kinds. Our government, through the Childrens'
Bureau, and individual state departments of public welfare
have developed a large network of public child welfare services. Along with these are many local child welfare agencies
supported by community funds and sectarian groups. As you
can understand, there is no group in our population to which
people's hearts go out so readily or for whom people's purses
open so widely as to helpless—and always hopeful—children. So the variety of services within child welfare is difficult to put into a nutshell.

The major kinds of child welfare service are these:

Under state auspices a great deal of work is done by caseworkers with parents and children in their own homes. There
is considerable overlap here with family welfare work, of
course, but usually the child welfare worker is called in when
one or more of the children in a family is actually being
badly neglected or mistreated. The caseworker in these instances tries to help the parents or parent work out such
physical, economic, or emotional problems as undermine their

ability to give their children the care and protection that they need.

When this doesn't work, when the parents are clearly unable to give decent care, the children may be taken from them for placement. Sometimes parents give them up voluntarily, even indifferently. Every day's city newspaper carries a story of parental neglect of children: the mother who has abandoned her infant; the parents who are trying to sell one of their children; the mother who frequents taverns for companionship and "blot-out" while her six-year-old "takes care" of the three younger children; etc. Social workers understand the deep psychological sickness that makes for so many of these situations, and when that sickness seems incurable, children may be put in placement for many years— sometimes till they grow up. In some cases they may be surrendered by their parents for adoption. In some they may be placed in foster homes where healthy and fond foster parents may begin to heal their psychological wounds. Sometimes these children are placed in institutions.

The day of the large institution where children were regimented and massed like little prisoners is, happily, on the wane—not waning fast enough, to be sure, but many new and fine institutions are being developed where children are given individual attention, sensitive treatment, schooling, and recreational advantages. Social workers are the chief planners and workers in these modern child-treatment institutions.

There are also those child-placement situations where parents deeply love and care for their children, but must turn to the child welfare agency for placement because sickness, usually mental, makes it impossible for them to give parental care, or because the child himself is too seriously disturbed to be able to live at home. Here, too, depending on the child's needs and resources, foster homes or institutions are used. In all child welfare agencies caseworkers have at least three areas of operation. They work with the children themselves, helping them to understand and to bear the separation from their own homes and to make the best possible adjustment to their new environments. They work with foster parents and housemothers and housefathers, helping them to understand and deal with the many emotional problems most of these children bring with them. They work with the child's own parents, toward helping them to release the child from unhappy bondage, or toward becoming better parents so that eventually they may reclaim their child.

Increasingly, child welfare institutions are using group workers as part of their treatment program. Sometimes the group workers are recreation directors, but far more often they work with those children whose life experiences have made them afraid of or hostile toward others, and help them learn to work or play in a group and to relate to other children and adults in reasonably appropriate ways.

The problems of childhood and adolescence seem to be growing in number and complexity these days. Or perhaps it is that people are more keenly aware than ever before that "how the twig is bent, so grows the tree" and "the child is father to the man." In any case the demand for trained caseworkers and group workers to deal with frightened and anxious or chronically angry and delinquent children is a growing and continuous one. Along with the demand for more social workers in this field is the demand for more knowledge and quicker, better means of treatment of the many variations of parent-child problems that social workers see today. So, in child welfare as in family welfare, there are many kinds of research and experimental efforts in progress.

In many communities family and child welfare agencies have come together and operate as one agency. You can see why. It is very difficult indeed to determine when a family-centered problem becomes a child-centered one.

Alongside these mergers is the development of many specialized family and child welfare agencies. For example, in more than one community you will find an agency specializing in problems of adolescents. In some you will find a nursery school set up for problem children, where teachers and family caseworkers work closely together. Another agency specializes in helping unmarried pregnant girls and women, providing the shelter and medical attentions they need, counseling with them on whether to keep or give up their babies, finding and selecting prospective adoptive parents. A project in yet another agency focuses on finding people who want to and would make good adoptive parents for children who have physical handicaps or children of mixed racial backgrounds. In several places there are agencies specializing in the migration and adjustment of refugees and displaced adults and children. Often they work closely with European agencies. Some family and some childrens' agencies are concentrating treatment and study efforts today on problems of young delinquents, and so forth. These basic social agencies—family and child welfare—are continuously involved in trying to find better ways of giving people the help they need. As a practitioner in such agencies, the social worker is not only a helper but often an experimenter, too.

Recreational Agencies

Thus far you have seen social agencies set up for problems so pressing and acute that they cry out for help. But there are also social agencies that are set up to prevent the occurrence of need, that offer opportunities for recreation and association with other people and for self-expression—agencies that may be said to be enrichers of people's environments. These are largely *group work agencies*—boys' clubs, neighborhood and settlement houses, "Y's," camps, community centers. Often they have a caseworker on their staff to deal with individual personalities who may disrupt group life or who are unable to handle themselves in a group. But chiefly they use group workers to provide the means by which people—adults as well as children—might re-create their work-a-day selves, stretch their horizons, facilitate wholesome associations with others. These agencies, when they are manned by professionally trained social group workers, offer not only the *place* where people can get together and the *materials* and *activities* that people can get involved in, but also the *leadership* that keeps in the forefront the idea that group activity is for the development of good communication and cooperation among the group members. The group worker's objective is that what is learned at the agency may be carried into living on the outside—into family relationships, work relationships, everyday neighbor and social relationships. You glimpsed something of all this when you

visited Bill Shepard's Center. To the casual eye a settlement
or neighborhood house or a group agency may seem just a
place where adults and children drop in to fill in time. But a
more careful observer will see, as you probably did, that all
these activities are chiefly the means by which people, young
and old, find themselves in relation to new interests and outlets and also to their fellow man.

Councils of Social Agencies

As soon as a community sets up several kinds of social
service and incorporates them into different agencies, the
necessity for planning and clearing among those agencies
becomes plain. It's evident, too, that there will be need for
fund raising and fair apportionment of community monies
among the various agencies. Such apportionment ought to
be decided by facts about what services are most needed,
which overlap and can be dispensed with, what gaps need to
be filled, and so on. In short, community planning and action
requires the development of *welfare councils, Community
Chests and councils, councils of social agencies*—all of them
for the purpose of planning, organizing, and supporting the
social services. Here is where the Don Freemans, the community organizers, work.

Much of the work of improving the social services, of calling attention to unmet needs, comes from study done by
social work researchers. They have had the problems placed
before them by the various agencies whose caseworkers and
group workers have their fingers on the pulse of the people
in the community. The front-line reports and suggestions of
caseworkers and group workers are usually relayed through

their agency's executives and directors to council committees for consideration and planning.

Actually, a council of social agencies or a community fund agency is not a direct service agency. It is rather a fund-raising, planning, and coordinating body, made up of representatives of service agencies plus representatives of other groups in the community. As you saw when you visited Don Freeman, its social workers are fact finders, appraisers, and planners in relation to community needs and problems; they are fund raisers, interest raisers, and coordinators of agency and citizen efforts to meet those problems.

Up to this point you have seen those agencies that are "primary" social agencies, that is, that are totally staffed by social workers (although they may use other professional persons as aides and consultants). But there is another large group of agencies which hire caseworkers and group workers for the particular competences they can bring. These are *schools, child guidance clinics, adult psychiatric clinics, psychiatric and general hospitals, and correctional agencies.*

A school to teach children the three R's, a hospital to mend broken bones, a clinic to restore mental health, and a court of law are very different kinds of places. You may well wonder what social workers do in all of them. But for all their differences these are all human welfare agencies, and they all have these reasons for needing and using social workers:

People aren't always able to use such opportunities as education or medical care that are available to them. They may be scared or blocked or ignorant. They often need help to talk over and work through the feelings or other obstacles

that make them unable to do such things as concentrate on
school lessons, face up to surgery, carry out the judge's
order, get out of bed and get dressed and say hello to the
man in the next bed. Some emotional quirk blocks them. Or
they may be blocked by other people or by circumstances in
their environment. An empty stomach is a poor base for a
child's learning. So is a state of continuous tension and
wrangling at home. A cold and indifferent family is a poor
prospect ahead of a mental patient whose doctor urges him
to "get well so that you can go home." The possible loss of
a job is a big deterrent to a man whose doctor advises him to
have surgery. And so on.

So whenever people seem unable, because of factors within
themselves or for any external reason, to use the educational,
legal, medical, and psychiatric services they need, social caseworkers are called upon to help them remove the emotional
or social obstacles.

Each of these places where social workers are part of a
team with another profession deserves some separate explanation.

Medical Social Work Departments

Hospitals of all kinds use social caseworkers as part of the
medical teams in the treatment of the sick. The establishment
of a medical social work department in a hospital means that
the doctors there have recognized that a patient is more than
his sickness. It means that one or more of the doctors in
authority have the conviction that "getting well" or adjust-
ing to chronic illness or even just following the doctor's

orders is greatly influenced by many factors in a patient's life.

One factor may be the patient's frame of mind, his feelings and attitudes about himself, his illness, the hospital, whatever. Another may be the patient's home situation—what's happening to his wife and children while he's in the hospital; or, if he's an out-patient, what circumstances at home—social, economic, interpersonal—underpin his recovery or undermine his strivings toward health. Being sick is sometimes a luxury, too. If wages are cut off or if medicines are costly, a patient may need help in making connections with social agencies that can provide assistance.

Then there are those situations where the illness of one family member can undermine the social and psychological well-being of the whole family. When, for instance, a mother is hospitalized and leaves helpless and worried children at home, or when she is bedridden at home and there is no one to cook supper or wash underwear or to say, "Now it's bedtime," a family's stability is likely to be shaken. Often friends or relatives may come in to fill the gaps and pick up dropped roles. But many families have no "natural" helpers, and in these cases the medical social worker acts to find the resources in the community (such as homemaker services) or to offer family members such moral support and release from their fears that they remain steady in the face of trouble.

Hospital and clinic social caseworkers (called "medical social workers" in these particular settings) typically give these kinds of help: They obtain the material means that a patient and/or his family may need for social, economic, physical, or psychological well-being. They deal with the actions and attitudes of people whose behavior affects the patient's welfare. They work directly with the patient himself, helping him to talk about and get free of anxieties or confusions or misapprehensions about himself, his family, his future; helping him to consider ways and means of coping with his handicap (if he has one) ; making arrangements for him with convalescent homes or rehabilitation centers. And they work with doctors and other staff people, helping them to know the social and psychological factors that have important bearing on the patient's illness and recovery.

The "where" of medical social work is in hospitals, big or small, and in out-patient clinics. On any one day you will be at a patient's bedside on the ward as he tells you about the letter from his wife full of her worries about money and the children's behavior. You will be in a doctor's office, discussing with him some of the reasons this patient doesn't seem to want to get well. You may be visiting the patient's wife, trying to lead her to some understanding of her husband's need for her courage and moral support. You may, in short, be in all the places where there is need for the understanding and handling of the social and personal problems that sickness brings.

Psychiatric Hospitals and Clinics

In hospitals for the mentally ill, in the wards of general hospitals set aside for mentally and emotionally disturbed patients, in clinics to which disturbed or distressed people— young and old—come, are social caseworkers called (again named by their setting) "psychiatric social workers." In recent years, with a rapidly growing interest in dealing with patients in groups as well as singly, psychiatric hospitals and clinics have begun to draw in social group workers, too.

In mental and emotional, as in physical, illness patients have to be helped to work at getting well, and whether they are ready and able to work at it is heavily influenced by the people to whom they're emotionally tied (their parents, spouses, children) and also by whether the life situation they have to cope with is too full of difficulty or is manageable.

The psychiatric social worker, like his medical social worker counterpart, is deeply involved in helping the patient himself and other people (members of his family usually) to cope with the difficulties in the environment that make living hard to handle or to face. These difficulties may be obvious, like too hard a job with too little gratification, or they may be subtle ones, like the interplay of feelings and attitudes between the patient and his intimates, feelings that create or feed his illness. Wives and husbands and parents and children, all of us really, find it very difficult to understand another person's emotional disturbance. Even when we understand it, it is extremely hard to live with and to bear. The moody or unreasonably hostile or frankly crazy behavior rouses all sorts of miserable feelings, not only in the mentally disturbed person himself but also in those close to him. Anger, resentment, guilt, anguish—all these and other emotions complicate an already unhappy situation. For the patient and his family, life becomes full of problems, hazards, and fears. Here are just a few expressions of them:

"How *can* I put my wife into an institution? She'll be so terribly unhappy there!"

"Yes, it's true that my son has shut himself up in his room for weeks and won't see anyone. But don't you think he's just—well, moody? I mean, no one in our family has ever had a mental breakdown!"

"It's impossible to keep this man at home! He goes into such terrible rages and threatens us and talks to himself, and the children and I are afraid for our lives."

"I know I should try—I know I should try to be interested —but everything inside of me says, 'Die, die, die.' "

"But we have no room in the house to take Father back! We moved into a smaller place when he went into the hospital four years ago—and now there's no place for him. Besides —he's still really not altogether 'there,' you know."

"Sure, I love him. But how long can a woman wait for a man to get well?"

"I don't know if I can get a job or not any more. I don't know if anyone wants me. I'm sort of scared to go out of here."

You can see what the psychiatric social worker is faced with and what he may have to do. Like the medical social worker, he deals continuously with the people whose lives are bound up with the patient, whose attitudes and actions affect those of the patient. Like the medical social worker, he gets the facts about the patient's social, economic, psychological circumstances which help to explain the nature of the illness or disturbance, and which may need to be taken into account in treatment. Like the medical social worker, he may work directly with the patient (in careful consultation with a psychiatrist), hearing out his problems, providing a warm and supporting safety island of relationship. He guides, leading the patient in small steps, often over long weeks of many interviews, to see more clearly, to feel more sure, and to cope with people and conditions outside himself.

The group worker in the psychiatric hospital or clinic works with several patients at a time, trying to get them to relate to him and to one another. This is because getting well and being well are largely made up of being unafraid of one-self and unafraid in relationships with other people.

Both psychiatric caseworkers and psychiatric group workers operate in a team relationship to one or more psychiatrists (heads of the team) and psychologists in clinical settings. In hospitals they work with many other professional people, too—nurses, occupational therapists, pharmacologists; the list is a long one. Today's psychiatric treatment centers are complex places because mental illness and emotional disturbances are complex conditions. The social worker is only one of the many professional persons bending their efforts to understand and deal with the mysteries of man's psychological health and sickness.

Child Guidance Clinics

The child guidance clinic specializes in the problems of young children. These clinics are set up sometimes as separate agencies and sometimes as parts of general or pediatric hospitals. The social caseworker here is called a psychiatric social worker, as in adult psychiatric settings.

Sometimes it is hard to say how the work of a child guidance clinic is different from a child or a family welfare agency. In any of these the caseworker may deal primarily with the parents or parent or primarily with the child. In the child guidance clinic the psychiatrist carries the basic treatment authority. Family and child welfare agencies that work with disturbed children always have psychiatrists as consultants to their casework staffs. So whether in a family agency, a child welfare agency, or a child guidance clinic, when a young child shows serious emotional or mental disturbance, both a social caseworker and a psychiatrist are usually involved. Their division of labor—who takes on the treatment of the child and who takes on that of the mother or mother and father—is worked out differently at different times and places and in relation to the case needs.

On one thing there is full agreement: For reasons that are not entirely clear, the children coming to child welfare agencies and guidance clinics today seem far more disturbed than the children of an earlier generation. Far more needs to be understood about the causes of their emotional disturbances in order that better treatments may be worked out. In this effort social workers, psychologists, psychiatrists, and others agree that all kinds of study, fresh ideas, and combinations of professional efforts are needed. Child guidance, which has such a pleasant and friendly sound, has become one of the most puzzling areas of need in both social work and psychiatry. Social workers are involved in it in almost every setting in which they work.

School Systems and School Social Work

Just as the medical social worker came into being when medicine discovered the "whole man," so school social work began when educators discovered the "whole child." It started when some teachers were concerned enough to make visits to the homes of children who were having troubles in the class-room or whose appearance and behavior gave indications that something was probably wrong. The usefulness of visiting teachers led to their development as one part of the school's responsibility to children. Most of the early visiting teachers lacked knowledge and understanding of the social-psychological problems of children; their training was largely, of course, in understanding children who came to learn and who were for the most part able to do so. Even those visiting teachers who deeply understood children lacked the background with which to deal with their family needs and situations which were so often at the bottom of the child's difficulty. More and more, social work training began to be called for. School social workers are the trained caseworkers who are adjuncts and aids to a modern school's educational program.

School social workers work with children who are referred by teachers and their families. The problems for which these children are referred run all the way from "no shoes," "no breakfasts," "family life is completely disorganized" to problems of emotional difficulties that are interfering with the child's learning or normal development. "Michael is a very withdrawn little boy—seems to be isolated from other children and to be living in a dream world," says one teacher. From another: "Fred is a potential delinquent—always fighting, always a chip on his shoulder—cheats without batting an eyelash. Yet his psychological tests show a very high I.Q." From another: "Betsy is continually absent. Says her mother is sick and cries all the time, and she, Betsy, must stay home and care for the younger children."

As you can see, every one of these referrals calls for someone to get the facts about the child, his family situation, and the reasons for the problem, and then to work out some plan for tackling the problem. The school social worker gathers this data, but because he usually covers a very large school or even a number of large schools, he cannot be the caseworker on all the situations referred to him. He does some preliminary interviewing wth teacher, child, parents—sometimes one, sometimes all—and then mobilizes other resources for cases that need intensive work. He acts as a link between school, child, family, and the welfare agencies, the relief agencies, the clinics, or whatever other social services seem to have relation to the problem.

With less serious problems, the school social worker may work with a boy or girl in the school office, talking over his problems, helping him to "get on the ball" again. He may also see parents in a guiding-advisory way over several interviews. He does a good deal of discussion with the teachers themselves, helping them to get perspective on some of their problem students and to cope with this or that bit of problem behavior. You may remember that Sue Fairchild, a family caseworker, led a discussion group for teachers in her district's school. If there had been school social workers in that particular school system, similar group discussions would have been carried on.

Not all school systems use school social workers. Some boards of education believe they cannot afford them. But as education increasingly recognizes the relationship between learning problems and problems inside the child and outside the classroom, the need for school social workers as links between school and home has become increasingly accepted.

Courts and Correctional Institutions

There was a time when courts meted out justice and its consequent rewards and punishments to all who came before them. Then came a day when it was recognized that reward and punishment decisions, if they were to be truly just had to take into account both the circumstances and the conditions that led to the problem and the consequences that would result from the judicial decisions. This was particularly apparent in cases involving child offenders, young delinquents, and parental neglect. Lawyers and social workers and prominent laymen brought about court reforms early in this century. Family courts and juvenile courts were established for cases that were heavily weighted with social and psychological problems, where rehabilitation seemed a possible outcome. In some places—unfortunately as yet in a minority of places—courts dealing with cases of families and children have taken social caseworkers onto their staffs. Their jobs: to get the facts about the problems and the people involved in the cases and to make recommendations to the judge about what ought to be done. ("This family seems able and willing to stay together provided supervision can be gotten from the Children's Agency." "This boy has been so long and consistently mistreated by his stepfather, and the latter seems himself to be so delinquent, that we recommend his removal from the home to an institution.") Often, beyond this, their jobs are to follow up on family neglect and delinquency cases and to get the services for them that will better the situation.

There was a time when probation—putting a person on a test of good behavior—and parole—putting a person who has been imprisoned on trial-freedom—were simply check-up, report-in systems. Today both probation and parole officers are increasingly seen as rehabilitation workers. In enlightened court systems they are seen as representing the court's benign arm and its helping hand. To the offender they say in effect, "I'm here to be of help to you. I'm here as the court's attempt to ward against repeating your mistakes— and more than that, to help you find outlets and aims that are satisfying to you *and* to our society." So you can see why social workers—or men and women with at least partial training in social casework—began to be wanted as probation and parole officers.

There was a time when young delinquents were sent to reform schools which were so poorly set up and so poorly staffed that they were scarcely schools at all, and any reforming that took place was often in the wrong direction. That time, sad to say, is still here. Most reformatories in most states of the Union are still barracks where boys, and sometimes girls, "do time." Yet, here and there are glimmers of light and change, enough to make one hopeful that with time and effort and money, the institutions that harbor delinquents can really become schools, learning places that reform, or refashion the motivations and behavior patterns of the young people in them. In those model correctional institutions, where the aim and the resources are to help young offenders become acceptable members of society, social caseworkers and sometimes social group workers work as part of the correctional team.

In short, as court and correctional systems become more socialized, more humanized, their use of social workers as part of their rehabilitation programs increases. But it is happening very slowly. Moreover, these are not easy places in which to work. The wheels of justice grind slowly, and sometimes to a caseworker eager for quick change, they seem to grind in cumbersome and blind ways. The young people brought into court and their families often seem to be hard nuts to crack, and it takes deep understanding and patience to stand by until they're ready to trust you. The conditions of work are often rough. But being brought to court is a point of no return for many youngsters, unless someone stands ready at that point to help reverse the vicious circle they're so often caught up in. Slowly but increasingly, social caseworkers are being drawn in to help "correction" mean not punishment but opportunity.

Other Places Where Social Workers Work

What you've been reading about so far are the main kinds of places where social workers work. But there is a growing recognition of social work and its relation to all kinds of human problems. So here are a few other kinds of organizations where you will find social work.

The United States Army uses men and women caseworkers in its Medical Service Corps, as psychiatric and medical social work officers. In its general and neuropsychiatric hospitals, its disciplinary barracks, reconditioning centers—at all points of undue stress or difficulty in military life—social workers commissioned as officers work in cooperation with medical and psychiatric officers.

Increasingly churches are hiring social workers for parishioner counseling, to staff church-supported institutions, and sometimes to bring church and community into closer working relationships.

Agencies that deal with crises in human life (Traveler's Aid, for example, working with lost and stranded travelers, runaways, etc.; or Red Cross with its relief operations during times of disaster) use many volunteers, but they depend on professional social workers for their backbone and supervisory staff.

Here and there "well-baby" clinics, prenatal clinics, and nursery schools use social workers as part of the regular staff or as part-time consultants on the family and mother-child problems that so often are first detected in these places.

As you can see, social workers work in almost any setting or organization that sets out to promote human well-being. Sometimes social work is the major profession, in charge of the whole operation. Sometimes it is a collaborating profession, adding a special dimension to the work of others.

For the most part, social workers are salaried employees of these social agencies or institutions. However, in the past ten years or so a small but growing number of social caseworkers have entered private practice. At this writing there are about twelve to fifteen hundred caseworkers in private practice. These are caseworkers with full professional training and a number of years of successful experience behind them. They have set up private offices of their own or together with several other social workers. Almost always they work in regular consultation with psychiatrists, who are often their chief source of case referral, and often in consultation with social worker colleagues. Their clients are people very much like those they've known before in social agencies, with many of the same kinds of problem, except that these clients must be able to pay fees for the counseling and guidance services they seek.

There have been some heated differences of opinion in social work as to whether private practice is "social." But only recently (1961) the Board of the National Association of Social Workers has given full recognition to the private practitioner in social work, stipulating, however, that he must identify himself clearly as a social worker. Requirements as to standards of schooling, experience, and expertness of such practitioners is presently in the association's committee work.

What all this says is that for a would-be social worker the question "Where shall I work?" leads to many answers. The choice may be limited at first, when you have but little experience or skill. But as your experience grows in depth and breadth and as you prove your competence, your choices and your chances will be over a wide and interesting range of places.

FIVE

How Do You Get to Be a Social Worker?

LET'S START WITH the assumption that you want to become a professionally prepared social worker. (Later we can talk about the jobs you can get without graduate education.) You will want to know what kinds of training and education schools of social work will expect of you; and also the qualifications required by the employment agencies.

Your Personality

To be a social worker requires that you be a certain kind of person. Sometimes when some of us old hands begin to line up specifications for the kind of person we want in the profession, we seem to be asking for saints, not human beings! But the fact is that there are some qualities a social worker just can't do without—and perhaps as they're set down here, you can do some self-analysis and ask yourself: Am I such a person?

First, a social worker must be more "people-oriented" than "thing-oriented." He must be concerned more with how people work than with how things work, and even when he thinks about things, it ought to be in relation to whether they are

108

good or bad for people. He must be more "action-toward-change" oriented than content with the status quo. Beyond being interested in people, he must have some fairly strong wish to help people struggle up and out of thir problems into a better life.

An interest in people means more than liking people or liking to be with them. It means a lively curiosity about all the ways people are and act, about their kindliness, their brutality, their depravity, their courage, about their smiling, sorrowing, hating, loving—all the emotions of that mysterious thing called personality.

Along with this interest must go real feeling for people. You should find in yourself some leap up of feeling with and for others, some sense that you are not only an observer of another person but a participator in his emotions. We call this empathy, which is to say you spontaneously put yourself into the shoes of another and know what he feels. You may feel compassion for him if he is in trouble, or you may feel at one with him in his happiness or triumph. There will, of course, always be some people you cannot identify with— someone who is cruel, a bully, a swindler—and social workers encounter such people, too. Then the social worker's professional discipline reminds him to "hate the sin but not the sinner," and he gives himself over to trying to understand what makes for the distortions and ugliness in this human being.

It would be a poor social worker indeed who could see only goodness in people, who had to deny (because he could not bear) human frailty. Human beings, all of them, you and I and all the people who come to social work, are "bad" as well as "good." An old popular song went "There's a little bit of bad in every good little girl!" That little bit of bad may grow big and permeate the human being's total personality under some unhappy circumstances and experiences. Or it may be a very minor part of our makeup because we've been lucky enough to have life experiences that have, as we say, brought out the good in us. Anyhow, this is why social work does not look for saints or Pollyannas as its practitioners (even if it could find them!). We hope you've got some "badness" in you. We hope you are aware of your badness, that is, that you recognize that right now, or at times in the past, you have had mean thoughts or wishes, maybe have done mean things, that you have felt urges to do many forbidden things, that you have felt hate, anger, envy—in short, that you have been a human being.

The point is that it is not possible to understand in another person what you have never known, in some small degree, in yourself. Therefore, a person must know himself in preparation for knowing others. The test of his ability to help others —to be a social worker—will be his capacity to recognize his own desires and urges, and then to contain and control them in order to use himself in service to another. This capacity is part of maturity. In the education of a social worker, his capacity to feel with and for other people and to manage his own feelings will be tested over and over again, and will be strengthened.

Beside interest in and feeling for people and self-management ability, a social worker ought to have in him a quick sensitivity to justice and injustice, to right and wrong, fair and unfair, especially as these values relate to the interaction between society and its members. You know this sensitivity in yourself when you see or hear of people being exploited, deprived, discriminated against, pushed under, etc. Social conditions that cut off people's rights to decent living conditions and undermine their self-respect should bother you whether you actually see them or only read about then in the papers. A good social worker never loses this "divine discontent" or his sense of social justice.

Beyond this righteous indignation should be some sense that you want to *do* something about the situation. Doing something may involve others than yourself—but at least you want to put a hand to the task. Doing something that is appropriate and effective will be surer and better directed once you've had the social work education that helps you know more about your society and the social resources, programs, and policies that affect so many people's lives. A social work education will give direction to your "divine discontent," but the spark of it must be in you.

Then there's that basic, all-important quality we call maturity. Everyone talks about it—but hardly anyone can define it. Maturity, for any given age, means something like this: Basically and usually you feel fairly steady, fairly secure. You feel more at one with your world than at odds with it. You feel reasonably able to cope with your life tasks. When you're frustrated or depressed—as who isn't at times?—you are able to bear it in the expectation that you'll get on top of that problem, too.

All of this, you'll note, is in relative terms—more rather than less, reasonably rather than ideally—because no one is totally mature all of the time. The point is that, as you've already seen, social work is a demanding profession. You will encounter in it problems that are shocking, harrowing, nagging, depressing. You will be working with people who are caught up in many conflicts and troubles and, therefore, emotions. And you've got to have built-in shock absorbers, which is what this elusive thing called maturity provides.

One part of these shock absorbers is humor. The trouble with humor is that you can't cultivate it: it's in you or it's not. When you've got it, it helps a lot. There are many very funny things that happen when you're working with people. But there are many frustrating things, too; and it's for these latter that you'll need the buoy of humor.

Patience is important, too. People and circumstances just won't change because a social worker says, "Presto!" Sometimes you'll have to cover the same ground with a person over and over again; often you'll have to take very small steps toward a far-off goal; sometimes your best-laid plans will flop like a house of cards, and you will need to plan all over again. (Go back and look at examples of this in Sue Fairchild's and Bill Shepard's and Don Freeman's day.) You must be willing to pace your steps to those of the people you work with; this is the necessity for any leader who is also a helper.

Do you rate reasonably well? If so, come along further.

Your Life Experience

When a young social worker faces himself honestly on some morning when he is to meet his clients, he sometimes has qualms and says to himself: Good heavens! What do *I* know about what a marriage relationship should be like? Or how a father should treat his delinquent son? Or what will this group of old people I am about to meet think when they see a callow youth like me? The student in schools of social work often asks himself these panicky questions: How can I, barely into my twenties, with a life experience that's been only school, school, and more school—how can I know about and help people with their problems? If I only had more experience . . .

It's true that most students are young and have a rather limited range of life experience when they enter a school of social work. But several other things are true, too. One is that you'd have to live a very long time to experience even a small part of the life patterns and problems that are brought to social workers. Another is that experiencing something doesn't necessarily mean one knows and understands it. (You know people who have had many experiences but who see them simply as "something that happened to me" and do not understand them at all.) The reverse may also be true: that it is possible to understand an experience deeply without having lived through it. This is possible, however, only for those people who have the ability we spoke of before—to give themselves over to feeling *into* and *with* other people—and who, further, always have their sensitive antennae out to get the meaning and the sense of what is happening within their own small life-space.

What I am saying is that it is possible to have many real and many vital vicarious experiences by the time you're twenty, even if you're leading a so-called "sheltered life." It's possible if you've got your "feelers" out.

First of all—you have been part of a family. You have experienced the interactions between yourself and your parents and sisters and brothers and other relatives. You have been an observer of their actions and interactions. You have known sickness, maybe even death, and their effects on people. You have known happy moments and unhappy ones, and you can think back across your own life history enough to understand something of childhood and early adolescence and the kinds of things that affected you. You know something of the problems and pleasures of making friends and getting along with people, and something of the ways in which people can hurt and disappoint or help and support one another. You have had at least some small sample of almost all the human feelings there are to be felt. And while it is true that there is only one *you* and the people in your world are relatively few, human beings are enough alike so that you are already equipped to understand a good deal about them.

There is one infallible way to expand your life experience. That is to read, read, and read. Read novels, old ones, new ones, American, English, Russian—it doesn't matter. But they should be good ones, because a poor writer writes about paper dolls in contrived situations, but a good writer writes about three-dimensional beings caught up in conflicts within themselves or with others. If you can feel with the characters in novels and plays, if what they feel and think and do holds your interest, then you are having a kind of experience that widens and deepens your understanding of people and human dilemmas. Those who read a great deal and with depth have the good luck to experience many lives, not just one!

One further practical way to widen your experience: If you are of college age, you may be able to find summer jobs that will give you some taste of what working with people is like. In a growing number of cities today, there are agencies interested in recruiting college students for social work careers.

They are part of a Careers in Social Work program and offer summer jobs that give you helpful orientation and some experience with social work practice. (See Chapter Seven. If there is no Careers in Social Work program in your community, there are these other possibilities: Camp counselor jobs, playground or nursery-school assistant jobs are often available. Some family and children's agencies, some public assistance agencies, some mental hospitals have summer job openings for college students, particularly for college students who think they may want to enter social work as a career. Of course, you're not likely to get the most interesting jobs in such agencies, since you'll have little experience or skill to offer—but you'll get a chance to get some first-hand impressions of yourself in relation to people and their problems and of what social workers deal with. (Chapter 7 tells where to look for such jobs.)

Your College Work

To be a professional social worker you must have a master's degree from an accredited graduate school of social work. The master's degree is given on your successful completion of two years (actually eighteen months) of classroom and practical experience, after you have gotten your B.A. or B.S.

To meet the entrance requirements of schools of social work, these requisites are important:

Courses: Most schools of social work will be more interested in the quality and pertinence of your college undergraduate work and activities than in the exact roster of courses you took. Most schools would agree that a liberal education, a humanistic orientation, offers the best base for what the social worker must be, know, and do.

Among the liberal arts and sciences are some subjects that bear very closely on social work. They are required by many schools, valued by all, but under any circumstances they offer you a chance to see for yourself whether the subjects that are highly pertinent to social work have real interest for you.

Psychology, social psychology, biology, sociology, social anthropology—courses such as these provide explorations and explanations of man in interaction with his environment. You can see why they would be important.

Economics and political science courses offer the basic knowledge on which to build your understanding of government and its social welfare responsibilities; of the great public programs that are this country's major social services; of how an affluent society can have pockets of poverty; of what politics and taxes and government spending have to do with the man-in-the-street who may be your client.

A course in statistics (don't groan!) offers you primary tools for grasping what social work researchers and planners are talking about when they are trying to find out, for example, how widespread a problem is, what percentage of people are affected, etc. Social planning depends on such assessments.

Literature and philosophy courses deepen your understanding of human beings in conflict and dilemma. Literature opens up ways of experiencing the lives of many other people; philosophy pushes you to think deeply about the human condition. Both of these explorations, in experiencing and thinking, will broaden and deepen the reservoir of understanding you bring to social work education. Courses in writing and speaking are immediately useful. Social work is totally dependent upon communication, so its practitioners must know how to make themselves simply and plainly understood, not only by their clients but by their colleagues, and especially by the community that supports their work.

Foreign languages, especially Spanish, will be very useful in some communities where a number of people who need assistance speak little or no English. In short, a good science, literature, and arts undergraduate background, plus whatever language skill you can offer, will stand you in good stead.

If you should lack a course or so that a social work school might require, don't worry. There are usually ways these deficiencies can be made up. By and large, as was said before, schools are chiefly interested in what you've done with the learning opportunities you have had.

A good rule: When you are ready to plan your junior year at college, write to several schools of social work (those that interest you because of their reputation, their location, or whatever), and ask for their catalogues. In these you will find their exact prerequisites stated; and in Chapter 7 you will find the names and locations of accredited schools.

In a number of colleges and universities today, courses in social welfare or social work are given as part of the bachelor's degree curriculum. In some colleges social welfare may be selected as a major, but this does not substitute for graduate work nor, if you took it, would you be eligible for membership in the National Association of Social Workers.

Schools of social work do not consider these undergraduate courses as prerequisite to their programs. Indeed there is some question as to whether or not a concentration of such courses in college rules out the range of liberal arts and science courses that are valued by graduate schools. The chief value in undergraduate social welfare courses is to give the interested undergraduate some information and foretaste of social work's subject matter, and, secondly, to offer some background for students who plan to do some casework or group work before they take their actual social work training. (The reasons for doing this will be discussed later in this chapter).

Grades: It is not possible to tell you what grade average you must have during your four years of college in order to enter a graduate school of social work. It varies. A few schools have all-university rulings about what grade average is the minimum for admission to any graduate school. Most schools are able to be flexible and will consider among other things the standing of the particular college that graded you (A's or C's aren't always equal to one another, we know). They will also consider the grades in the subjects that relate most closely to social work; the circumstances in your student situation (such as working your way through school) that might have affected your scholarship.

But grades are not enough. Qualities of personality and your college interests and associations will be carefully considered for whatever light they throw on your ability to invest your energies outside yourself and your freedom to work and play together with other people.

Schools of social work aren't intent on getting only one kind of person. The fact is that many schools today are trying to study carefully who makes the best social worker, and what relation exists, for example, between academic success

in college and success as a social worker, and between college
activities and social work, and, beyond this, whether caseworkers, group workers, and community organizers can be
cut from the same cloth. Social work educators are sure they
want a wide range of personalities, once the qualities men-
tioned at the beginning of this chapter are found to be
present, and once the undergraduate grades give evidence
that the student can cope with what will lie ahead of him.

Your Graduate Work

In the second half of your junior year at college, you
ought to begin thinking about where you'd like to go for
your graduate work in social work. By the fall of your senior
year you should have made the choice of the one or two
schools to which you plan to apply. Your application should
be in by January of your senior year (or of the year in
which you hope to enter a school's fall program). Later
applications are acceptable, of course, but early acceptance
in the school of your first choice, scholarship grants, etc.,
go to the early bird. More on this later.

There are over sixty accredited schools of social work today in the United States (including Hawaii and Puerto
Rico) and Canada (their names and locations are in Chapter 7). Some are relatively new schools, some old and long
established; some are small, some quite large; some are in
small college towns, some in big city university centers. Some
have fairly high tuitions, and some (state university schools)
have low tuitions for in-state students. Your choice will be
affected by considerations of where you'd like to be geographically, school size and cost, and the descriptions of

courses and aims you will find in their catalogues. You may also want to know about a school's reputation and standing (even though it is fully accredited). This information is a little harder to get, but your best bet is to discuss choices with any professional social workers you may know, and with the sociology or other advisory faculty in your college. While it is true that graduation from certain schools has greater "prestige value" than from others, it is also true that an M.A. or an M.S. in social work from any accredited school opens the same doors—and many of them—to job opportunities.

When you have some idea of what school of social work you'd like to learn about, write to the dean or director for a catalogue. A careful reading of a school's catalogue gives you not only the facts noted in the paragraph above, but other facts, too, such as the particular advantages of setting a school may have, the social agency connections it uses for student field work, the scholarship of its faculty, and so on. By these factors, too, your choice may be affected.

Application

Wherever you apply, it is important that you apply early. This is because all schools of social work are now having an increase in applications, and all schools of social work, though they would like to take all qualified applicants, must limit their enrollment. Enrollment is limited by the number of openings that social agencies are able to provide for the students' field work, and when there are no more such field placements open, a school cannot take more students.

A second reason for being an early bird is that while all

schools have scholarship funds, no school has enough to meet all requests. (Scholarships will be discussed further on).

Schools of social work are suffering from the same application problems that plague undergraduate colleges today —the multiple applications of one student to many schools. (Of course, that one student is only trying to leave no stone unturned in his motivated effort to achieve his goals!) But it becomes a costly process for a number of schools to go through the machinery that admissions procedures involve so that one student can go to one school. Therefore, deans and directors of schools of social work would probably be in agreement that the prospective student should be asked to make as careful a pre-application choice as possible. Then apply to the two—at the most, three—schools that most appeal to you for your own good reasons. If your applications go in early enough, you will be notified soon enough of your rejection (should that happen) to be able to apply elsewhere.

When you get your application blanks, you will find certain kinds of information asked of you. You will be asked for transcripts of your college record so that the courses you've taken and the grades given can be examined. You will be asked to give the names of people who would be willing to write reference letters about you. These should be people who have known you fairly well in their capacities as your teacher or employer or professional acquaintance.

Many schools will ask you to write some account of how you happened to become interested in social work, or what expectations you have of the field and of yourself in relation to it. Give this some careful thought. (One of the purposes of this book is to provide you with the food for such thought.) Try to write as honest and as open a statement as you can. Write a "this is what I, John Jones, am, want, feel, think" sort of answer rather than one of those "this is what I suppose you people want" letters. In the first sort of approach you come alive, you become a *person* for the people reading admission applications. In the latter approach you remain vague, dim, just another applicant. To show yourself as a person is important to a profession where so much hinges on interpersonal relationships.

Many schools like to have personal interviews with applicants. Of course, geographical distance often makes this impossible, and your inability to come for a personal interview will not stand in your way. To have your own questions answered, however, and to get some first-hand impressions of a school, you yourself might want to have a personal appointment with someone on the school's staff. Schools are glad to arrange for this.

Scholarships and Tuition Grants

All college and graduate work is expensive these days, and graduate work in a school of social work is no exception. Many parents today recognize that a bachelor's degree is no longer the entry to a vocation that it once was—and so they have planned and are ready to finance their young sons and daughters into graduate schools. If, however, financing is a problem for you, there are numerous possibilities for scholarship aids.

Most schools of social work give scholarship grants. Some cover full tuition plus expenses; some, tuition and partial expenses; and some, partial tuition only. The United States Government, state governments, individual states, and individual agencies are willing to pour an astonishing amount of money into the education and preparation of good social workers. The need for social workers is great, and their usefullness is widely recognized. Many agencies give scholarships on condition that the recipient will pledge a year or two of work in those agencies following his graduation. Others give scholarships free of commitment in order to build up the manpower of professional social work.

Every school's catalogue will tell you what particular scholarships and tuition aids it has to offer. Also, the Council on Social Work Education puts out a compilation of information about all social work education scholarships and money grants. (See Chapter 7).

Don't count on working while you're in a school of social work: it's possible but very difficult. A few students do manage it—if they have great energy and great self-discipline and are lucky enough to find a job that fits into a tight schedule. But you will find going to a school of social work consumes more time and energy than you were accustomed to using in undergraduate work. This is partly because your practice "field work" may take you far off campus, but it is mostly because field work can take a lot of your physical and emotional energy. There are a few instances where field work can be combined with earning money. (There will be many opportunities to get a summer job in social work between your first and second year of school.) But, by and large, schools encourage students to put themselves wholly and fully into the study of theory and practice that work in a professional school requires.

Now you have been accepted by the school of your choice.
You will usually be asked to decide which method of social
work you want to major in—group work (like Bill Shepard), casework (like Sue Fairchild), or community organization (like Don Freeman). (Social work research is not
open as a major to students in the master's program. Gen-
erally this preparation is part of the doctoral program.) If
you are uncertain as to which social work method you're
most interested in or fitted for, you'll be helped to think
through to some choice by someone on the school's faculty.
If you make a choice and find out early enough that it's not
right for you, it will be possible to work out a shift, in conference with your faculty advisors.

Ahead of you lie two years of study and practice toward
your master's degree in social work. In prospect it seems a
long time. You'll find it flies by breathlessly, so make the
most of it right from the first!

The Curriculum in Social Work

The reason it takes two years for a master's degree in
social work, while this degree may be won in many other
fields in one year, is this: Classroom courses in social work
are combined with actual practice in the field. All the kinds
of agency you read about in Chapter Four collaborate with
schools of social work to provide placement for students. In
these agencies, social work students spend approximately
half their time—about two and one half to three days a week
—with the other half devoted to class courses.

The student caseworker (or group worker or community

worker) carries cases (or groups or projects) with all the responsibilities of a staff social worker but on a more limited scale and with closer supervision. In your field work you will try to apply and test all your class- and book-learned theories and principles. You will be finding that they "come true" with increasing frequency and deepened meaning for you. You will be putting your fast-growing knowledge to use in the service of people, learning to lend your eyes and ears and whole self to understanding, motivating, and assisting the people who are your clients. The constant safeguard that the school and the agency provide for you—and for your clients, too—is the guidance, instruction, and constructive criticism of an experienced social worker who will be your field work instructor.

It is not enough, as you can understand, for a student of social work to be academically competent. He must be this, too, but it is necessary that what he is learning with his head be continuously transferred to his heart and his hand. He not only must *know* but must be able to *do*. So the student of social work is always being appraised by the quality of his classroom performance (which he is accustomed to) and also by his ability to put his knowledge to use.

Schools of social work that are in or near cities divide the week between in-school classes and off-campus field work. Schools that are located in small communities with no range of social agencies use block placements. This means that they concentrate classwork on campus for several months at a time and then place students for months at a time in neighboring or far-off agencies. Each system has its advantages and disadvantages. Because it's not possible to say for a fact which is better, this consideration probably ought not to enter into your decision about what school to choose.

You will spend your first year's field work in one agency. In your second year you will go to another type of agency, so that your experience of people and problems and social work places will be broadened. If you are a casework student, for example, you may spend your first year in a family welfare agency—public assistance or one of the voluntary family service agencies. In your second year you may choose your area of special interest—medical social work, advanced family casework, psychiatric social work, child welfare, and so on—and you will be placed in an agency in whose specialty you have particular interest. (A study of the catalogue of a particular school will tell you what kinds of agency that school uses for its teaching centers.)

Your field work days will give you an immediate experience of what it's like to be a social worker—you won't have to wait two years to find out. You'll experience what it's like to carry the responsibilities of helping other people. (But give yourself time on this! You can't feel secure about it or do all the right things right from the start!) You'll experience what a social agency is like as a place and as a purpose. You'll have contact with many people besides your fellow students—other social workers, clerical people, psychiatric and medical consultants, administrators, as well as many people in the community outside. Your closest relationship will be with your field instructor (often called supervisor) who will be teaching and helping you and will always be in touch with the school about your progress.

On your "school days" you will be in the classroom, taking

a sequence of courses designed to give you the foundation knowledge for social work. You may as well know now that there is not much free choice or many electives in a professional school's curriculum. Sometimes students who have enjoyed the freedom of range and choice in a liberal arts curriculum find themselves annoyed that in a school of social work they are required to take certain courses in a certain order, and that there's rarely time or space in their programs to sample attractive courses in other parts of the university. But this is a fact of life in any professional school: You are being prepared to be a member of a profession, and you are therefore required to take and to pass through its agreed-upon core of knowledge. A professional degree certifies that you have been taught, and have given evidence that you have incorporated, certain facts, theories, values, and skills. So with that firm (grim?) understanding, what will your course work consist of?

You will take a group of courses about the nature of man in society. There will be one sequence of courses (called by different names in different schools, and with some differences of emphasis, but all aiming toward the same end) on man as a bio-psycho-social organism. You will learn about the psychological and social implications of physical illness; about how personality and behavior develop and are shaped by physical, emotional, and social interactions.

In courses in casework (or group work or community work, depending on your major) you will study the dynamics of social interactions, with special emphasis upon the interaction between the social worker and his client and on the principles that govern enabling and therapeutic methods and skills. You will be learning and considering issues in the ethical and value systems that underlie the practice of social work.

This cluster of courses has to do, in short, with human behavior in our particular society, with the social problems and interactions that mold and shape that behavior, and with professional social work's problem-solving processes. All these courses will have immediate bearing upon what you will be doing in your field work.

A second major cluster of courses in all schools of social work has to do with the organization and nature of the social services. From these courses you will learn of the development of social work and social resources for the meeting of certain kinds of human need, the kind of provisions that have been developed to meet the economic, mental, and physical health, child welfare, and rehabilitation needs of people in our society.

You will study not simply what these are but how they meet, or fail to meet, the social, physical, and psychological welfare of people; how politics and policies affect these services and what your state legislators and your congressman and your particular community have to do with them; what kinds of action are needed to make them better than they are; and what social workers have to do with making them more efficient and effective. You will find many questions of basic philosophy and social values involved, as well as many as yet unresolved issues; so here, too, as in your methods courses, you will learn the facts by which to form your social opinions and will think about social action on the basis of these facts and opinions.

In your field work, of course, you will be working in one kind of social service, a particular kind of social organization. Your courses in the social services should give you some perspective about where your agency stands in relation to social needs and to social provision, and should give you ways of thinking about your agency's history, source of support, policies, and procedures. All these affect your client and what you do with and for him.

Another concentration of courses is in social research—courses that help you to learn and understand the basic conditions that must be met for valid fact finding and investigation of problems important to social work, and that give you some elementary practice in doing a piece of research. The intention is not to make a researcher of you; this would hardly be so easily achieved. The idea is rather to make it possible for you to spot and be able to formulate some of the problems in your profession that need to be studied, and to have some general idea as to what would be involved in making a study. Along with this, your courses in "social investigation" (or some equivalent title) aim to help you to become an intelligent "consumer" of research. Every day's newspaper reports on somebody's study that "proved" this or that, on some percentages or statistics that "show," for example, that employment is up or down, delinquency is more widespread in this group than in that, more fraud occurs in relief families than . . . etc., etc. The point is that public opinion is shaped and colored by these "facts" that are sometimes only half facts, and social programs are aided or hampered by them. The professional social worker ought to know how to read such "facts, figgers, and data," ought to be able to put a finger on where fallacies lie, if they are there, or to know what questions are yet to be answered. The social sciences, psychological and medical laboratories, and social work's own research centers are pouring out findings of all kinds today that bear upon social work's programs and individual clients. How to appraise and use them is what your research sequence sets out to teach you.

Different schools at different times will have different single courses in their curriculums. Sometimes they are extra electives, sometimes required. But all schools of social work are agreed that their core courses are these that have been described and that give you knowledge on: man's makeup; his social interaction and functioning; the problems he creates or encounters; societal programs and provisions for man's needs; the processes social work has developed for solving the problems of man in society; the ways by which man's social welfare needs and the social services may be examined and appraised.

As I've presented these courses, it sounds as if they all come at once. They could not, of course. They extend over the two years' time, as you will see when you study school catalogues.

It's not all work and no play while you're attending a school of social work. At many schools, students form clubs that manage to provide both social work forums and social play. It's still possible to be involved in personal life and fun in campus activities, and to take advantage of the rich and varied cultural opportunities that are to be found in so many university communities.

Then on one day you'll be in that black gown with that

awkward-fitting mortarboard balancing on your head again, being presented by your school for the university's M.A. or M.S. degree. The probability is that you will already have a job in your pocket. It's usual that in the last six weeks or so of your second year you will find out from your field work agency and from your faculty advisor about job openings, or, as is often the case, you will have been found and interviewed by some agencies eager for trained and competent staff.

When you decide on "where," you'll find that there is a new beginning to make, new challenges, and that maybe you don't know as much as you wish you did. But you can surely know that at the very least you've gotten a firm base from which to learn and grow further.

Social Work without Training

Now—suppose you aren't sure yet whether you want to give yourself over to training for social work, or that you feel you want to mature a bit first, or that you can't afford to go on to school until you earn and put by some money. It is possible to be a social worker after graduation from college. From the point of view of what you can bring to the job and to the people you'll serve and from the point of view of what you can get out of the job, it is not truly desirable to be an untrained social worker. But it is possible.

It is possible because there is today a need for about ten times as many social workers as there are professionally trained people. By and large, the public assistance agencies throughout this country and many of the public child welfare agencies are staffed by people who have no formal education in social work or who have only partly completed such education. Probation officers are largely untrained or only partially trained workers. Many recreation workers have had no post-college work. So there are jobs to be had as case-workers, case aides, and group workers in many agencies today. (See Chapter 7 for details about this.)

In most large agencies that hire people directly from college, particularly those agencies that are part of state welfare departments, there are in-service training short-courses, often given by the agency's supervisory personnel, some of whom are professionally prepared social workers. In almost all such agencies there is encouragement to young casework-ers to take a part-time course or two in a school of social work (if there is one near by). Frequently, there are opportunities offered in the form of scholarships to a school of social work for one year and sometimes for the full master's program. The requirement is that you be a promising social worker; the expectation, of course, is that you will return to your supporting agency to give it the benefit of your learning.

Should you undertake a social work job without social work education, you must remember, of course, that you will not be assigned to one of the choice or more responsible jobs in the agency. You may be called a caseworker or a case aide, and certainly at first you will probably be heavily laden with many routine and onerous tasks. Remember, too, that you will not be seeing social work practice at its best for many reasons, including the important fact that most of your colleagues will, like you, be neither professionally trained nor committed. Your salary level is likely to be lower than a professionally trained person's even if he is doing much the same job, because merit system examinations (given for most public agency jobs) give higher ratings to the person who brings knowledge to the job. For that same reason, if for no other, the person with at least some graduate school work is likely to advance first and faster.

Nevertheless, there may be some real advantages to you in a job in social work if you cannot, or are not sure you want to, go directly on to graduate school. You will have the firsthand experience of all kinds of people in all kinds of trouble. You will be able to know and assess in yourself whether you are interested and willing to give yourself over to helping others in the best way you can. You will inevitably mature a bit in the process of working and of growing a year or two older. You may be able to save money for later schooling. You may be lucky enough to have a supervisor or administrator who is able to teach you and enhance your skills. You may be recommended for one of the agency scholarships to a school of social work in order to become a leadership person in the agency and the field. And if, as you work, you are doing everything you can to meet people's needs and lessen their hurts, then it will be an advantage to the people you serve, too, that you are there.

But for them or their future counterparts, and for your own sense of identity and status and competence, hold before yourself the goal of full professional training.

When you are ready to consider the alternatives—schooling first, then work, or work first, then schooling—think them over carefully. Then talk them over, either in person or, if that's not possible, by letter, with the school of social work of your choice. Admissions personnel in schools of social work, remember, are almost always social workers themselves. That means they give individual attention and thought to the questions prospective students pose.

Perhaps you have one more big question. It's the title of the next chapter.

SIX

Why Be a Social Worker?

DOES IT SEEM to you rather late in this book to be asking this question? I've held it until now on the notion that first you'd want to know the facts of what you'd be getting into if you chose social work as your profession. Now that you have some general idea—what's in it for you? What are the personal satisfactions and opportunities it offers?

Let's talk first about the disadvantages. You will never get rich in social work. The great majority of social workers are and always will be salaried employees—and since their salaries come from taxes or from community contributions, you can understand why they are within the modest to adequate range. (If you're still interested, there's data further on about actual salary ranges and advancement chances.)

Secondly—and this, too, affects the salary range—social work does not have the prestige and status of some other professions, particularly law and medicine. The reasons for this are varied: Social work's youth, for one. It was only forty years ago that a University first opened its doors to a graduate school of social work as a recognized professional school (the University of Chicago). Social work has had to live down its ancestral reputation as a volunteer's "do-gooder" occupation. The fact that the public meets so many social workers who still have not had professional education, and identifies all social workers with them is another reason for social work's lack of status. The fact that many people still think that social work is only for the morally or socially "inferior" and thus that social workers themselves bear some taint may be another reason. But for whatever reasons, social work has not been the community's favorite child.

Should you become a social worker, you will find that you are often having to explain yourself and your profession to other people—sometimes to hostile ones, sometimes to friendly ones. You will have to explain "just exactly what is it you do" time and again. You will interpret over and over that all people who are poor are not, a priori, cheats and chiselers. You will find yourself at a dinner party explaining to the person on your right why social workers deal with the social problems of middle-class people as well as of the poor, and to the person on your left why social workers must champion the rights of the underdog. In short, social work is frequently under fire and challenge, and it calls for conviction and clarity in its practitioners to win it prestige.

Oddly enough, though, communities and community leaders clamor for social workers more than ever before! Of this, more further on.

Finally, among social work's disadvantages, is the fact that social work is not an easy job: it's not a nine-to-five proposition, though these may be your actual working hours. A social work job takes a lot of energy, physical and psychological, if only because of the self-discipline that is involved in dealing with a great variety of people who are so often under stress or in crisis. Its problems may wake you in the middle of the night, when you may start up thinking: Heavens! I should have done this—or that! Or: I wonder if Sally really *did* go home instead of to her boy friend's. Or your involvement in some social-political issue or some agency problems may keep you at a committee meeting far into the night. So at many times social work requires that you be able and willing to extend yourself beyond yourself.

Are you still with me? If so, we can talk now of some motivations and rewards in the social work profession:

Interest

It is simply impossible for a social worker to be bored. The variety and interest and emotional impact of people of all ages, all backgrounds, involved in all the problems or the striving, all the hurts and the needs of human beings—this in itself keeps the social worker's daily job a lively, fascinating one. You are always with people, always related to life and living. Your work will bring you into contact and into working relationships with a number of other professional persons, too—chiefly doctors, psychiatrists, teachers, often psychologists, lawyers, and various community leaders interested in one of your clients or one of your projects. Social workers often echo Bill Shepard's cry, "Oh, for a good, dull, monotonous day!"

Service

As a social worker you are an instrument of potential help and change for the better in the lives of many people. They can and often do gain physical, mental, emotional, and sometimes even spiritual nourishment and strength from you and from the resources you can make available to them. There are many failures and disappointments in the outcome of a social worker's efforts, it is true, just as there are many sicknesses a doctor can do nothing about. But you will feel repaid, warmed in heart, when people respond to your help in ways that tell you they feel better as a result of your help, or more capable of shouldering their own load. A smile that breaks across the face of a child whose inner tensions had once frozen him, a grudging but sincere "thanks a lot" from a troubled adolescent, a former psychotic patient who says, "I'm not afraid to go home to my family now," a group that has learned to govern itself and put its combined energies into constructive action—all and any one of these are rich rewards to the social worker. They say that you, in some small way, have helped someone to be and to do better.

"To serve" is probably the most important motive in social work—to reach out a hand to a fellow man—whether in one's own country or in a foreign land, whether on a person-by-person basis or through planning and execution of community reforms. When that service or help yields some fruitful results, even modest ones, the feeling of being lined up on the side of human-ness and of man's welfare is a deeply satisfying one.

The Need

There are eight to ten social work jobs open to every graduating student of social work. (A recent report from Washington projects the anticipated need for 44,500 additional trained social workers by 1970 in the public assistance, child

welfare, and delinquency control programs alone.) The fact
of the matter is that at least during your lifetime there will
always be need for trained social workers and many jobs
open to them. This is because there are recurring disasters
and crises that cannot always be foreseen or avoided—floods,
fires, business recessions, or the uprooting and movement of
masses of people due to political or social pressures. (Just
before this was written, for instance, West German authori-
ties were calling for doctors, nurses, and *social workers* to
meet the needs of the East German refugees, and at this
writing social workers are being called for in southern areas
devastated by the latest hurricane.) Social workers manned
—and still man—refugee and displaced-person operations
in Europe and the Far East all during and after the last
war. In many large cities here in the United States the heavy
immigration of southern and Puerto Rican families, white
as well as Negro, pose troubling problems for the communities and for the migrants themselves—problems that call for
social work's skill. Even in an affluent society there are shifts
and changes in the economic situation—technological
changes, for instance, that create economic and therefore
social and psychological crises for great numbers of people.
Their voices are listened to, their needs met, their futures
planned for, by social workers.

Another reason for the growing need and demand for social workers is that, unreasonable as it may seem, the more
a society meets the basic bread and shelter needs of its citizens, the more aware people become of their right to "life,
liberty, and the pursuit of happiness." That is, people begin
to look up from their stomachs to say "there are other rights

I have, too"—such as the right to expect happiness in marriage or the right to expect that there will be opportunities to develop oneself and one's children beyond keeping body and soul together. Social workers are sought to provide services beyond the food and shelter level: to provide counseling to help parents to be better parents, children to be better students; to provide recreational possibilities for adults and children; and so on. In short, so long as we live in a society that holds that the human being has a right to the pursuit of a personally satisfying and socially effective life, that society will want social workers, among its other professions, to make this goal possible.

Job Opportunities

Chapter 4 told you where social workers work; there will be job opportunities open in almost all of these places if you have a master's degree in social work. (Of course, how *many* agencies want you and how *much* they want you will depend also on your performance in class and field work during your student days.) Beginners usually take jobs as caseworkers or group workers, and occasionally as community organizers. Such jobs will be open to you in family and children's agencies, hospitals, psychiatric clinics, school systems, courts, children's institutions, community centers, and councils of welfare agencies. They will be open in all parts of this country and its far-off places (Alaska, Hawaii, Puerto Rico), in Canada, and sometimes (though usually these jobs are for experienced social workers) in foreign countries.

In the several pages that follow you will find some actual job advertisements for group workers, caseworkers, and community workers that appeared in social work publications this year. (I've omitted the exact locations and agencies, but otherwise the ads are as printed.) Notice that even for those positions that suggest the need for considerable experience, you could be qualified within five years after getting the master's degree. (MSW means Master of Social Work.)

Group Work

Social Group Workers (Male and Female). Biracial, mobile, decentralized, nonsectarian social work agency providing intensive direct service to small groups of emotionally disturbed and/or socially deprived boys and girls. Clients are referred for service by local health and welfare community resources. Intensive professional supervision, in-service training, and consultation. MSW required; no previous experience necessary. Liberal personnel practices. Starting salary $5,500 with minimal annual increments at $200.

Group Worker. For new type of neighborhood organization work under supervision of well-established settlement. Creative opportunity in helping neighbors maintain and improve advantages of urban living. Required: MSW and minimum of two years' experience. Beginning salary up to $6,000, depending on experience.

Group Worker (Male). In residential treatment center for emotionally disturbed children aged 6-12. Work with small groups in treatment-oriented group work program, some supervisory responsibility. Excellent supervision, psychiatric consultation. Required: MSW, experience in direct work with small groups. Salary $4,800-$7,000; initial salary based on qualifications.

Group Worker (Male preferred). For residential treatment center for 24 children, aged 5-12. To supervise a thera-
peutically oriented group work program through other staff
and volunteers; integrated with collaborative efforts of multi-
disciplined staff; supervision and training of child care staff.
Requirements: MSW in group work; experience necessary
but length of experience secondary to quality. Excellent
health and welfare benefits. Salary range $6,000-$7,500.

Casework

Child Welfare Services. Several openings in public
agency with a broad program of special services to children
including adoptions, services to parents and children in their
own homes on a protective basis, foster home licensing and
placement. Requirements: 1 year's graduate study in social
work, no experience. Salary, $6,084-$6,708.

Male Caseworker, MSW. To work with fatherless boys
and volunteer Big Brothers. Salary $5,200-$7,000. Position
offers many cultural and professional contacts.

Female Caseworker, MSW. To balance male staff; family
counseling and adoption program, or specialize in either
area. Professional freedom. Salary $5,500-$8,000 in either
area. Month's vacation, nine holidays, retirement, Social Security, paid insurance, etc.

Psychiatric Social Worker for well-established community
mental health clinic in stimulating university setting. To
assist in program development and the treatment of selected
alcoholics. Clinic employs multidiscipline approach, is psy-
choanalytically oriented, and has teaching affiliation with
the university. Opportunity to establish on-going social work

research, to do intensive individual and group treatment, and to participate in community organization. Liberal personnel policies, five weeks' annual vacation, Social Security, and retirement program. Opportunity for private practice. Can start $7,500, depending on qualifications.

School Social Workers (5). Well-established social work department, MSW required. Services provided include: social work evaluation of case situations which involve academic and/or social maladjustment, short-term treatment, casework with hard-to-reach families; authoritative casework with delinquent individuals and gangs; and intensive casework with emotionally disturbed children. School system has outstanding special services program including medical, psychological and special education services. School guidance service also available as well as community social service resources. Casework supervision provided. Interdisciplinary consultation available. Salary for 38-week work year: minimum, $5,360, maximum, $8,200. Excellent retirement plan, Social Security, group life insurance and health insurance benefits.

Community Organization

Executive Director (Male preferred). Immediate opening, for fast-growing area. Required: MSW with major in community organization, minimum 1 year's administrative experience, plus capacity to provide leadership and interpretation to professional and lay groups. Blue Cross, Blue Shield provided. Member of Health and Welfare Retirement Association. Starting salary $6,500 with yearly increments.

Community Social Worker. For voluntary national health organization. Public and professional education; chapter formation; counseling and referral. MSW with CO sequence required, experience, community skills, ability to work independently desired. Hospitalization and life insurance. Starting salary $8,500.

Community Mental Health Consultant. Participate in developing policies and procedures for a statewide mental health program; assume leadership in organizing groups, both lay and professional, in order to develop community mental health programs; provide professional consultation to agencies, institutions, and professional groups. Minimum qualifications: MSW with 5 years of professional experience including 1 year in administrative or supervisory capacity, remainder in consultation, community organization, and clinical work in mental health setting. Salary $7,560-$9,360, with beginning salary up to $8,280 possible.

After you have had at least three years' experience, preferably more (and depending, of course, on how capable you've been), many other jobs open up to you. Supervisory positions where you teach younger workers or students, executive or administrative jobs as director of small agencies or of an agency department, special demonstrations or experiments in practice—all of these wait to be filled by competent, experienced social workers. Increasingly, though in small numbers still, social workers are returning to school after (a minimum of) three years in practice to work toward an advanced degree—a Ph.D. or a Doctor of Social Work. Such study is for those who are particularly interested in social work research and in preparing for teaching in a school of social work. Perhaps it should be explained that, with rare exceptions, schools of social work do not allow students to go straight through from master's to doctoral work. There is general agreement that a Ph.D. degree in social work must mean more than scholarly competence. It must also mean that the holder of that degree has experience in putting the knowledge to use, as well as the theoretical knowledge itself. Therefore, successful practice as caseworker, group worker, or community worker is a prerequisite to becoming a doctoral student.

Many social workers prefer not to supervise or "administer" because they most enjoy the direct work with their clients, individuals or groups. The practitioner is, indeed, the lifeblood of any profession. As agency boards have grown to recognize this, salary adjustments have been made so that today many agencies have no difference between their top practitioners' salaries and those of their supervisory or administrative staff, and the social worker who wants to continue as a caseworker or a group worker may do so without loss of money or prestige.

If you have completed your college work and want a job in social work, either to try out the field or because you must wait and save before you can go on to get your master's degree, there will still be many openings for you. Public assistance agencies almost always need caseworkers or case aides or investigators, as the name may be. Courts want probation and parole workers. Recreation agencies hire untrained group and recreation workers. (For where to apply, see Chapter 7.) Your salary will, of course, be less than that of your professionally prepared colleagues. Your working arrangements will be less satisfactory. You will have a narrower choice of places in which to work because most agencies, certainly those that deal with people's maladjustments due to psychological factors, will not hire social workers without professional education. But the need for such help and understanding and hope as you can give, even as an untrained worker, is a deep and urgent one, indeed. In this country today you will find families on relief living in homes as primitive and deprived as those in far-off "have-not" countries. You will find parents with as little idea of how to feed and raise their brood of children as peasants in remote corners of the earth. There is, I believe, no Peace Corps mission more urgent and vital than that of the social worker who undertakes to help the masses of "downtrodden" right here in this country.

In short, when you enter social work, you enter a field where there is a growing, continuous, and pressing need for you and where there will be many kinds of job opportunity, especially if you are professionally prepared, in many kinds of agency.

Salaries and Fringe Benefits: By the time you read this there may have been a rise in social work salaries. The last ten years have seen a rapid rise, especially for the professionally trained worker.

In 1959 the National Association of Social Workers recommended to the field of social work that the beginning salary for an inexperienced graduate from a school of social work should be $5,400 per year; further, that the expectation be that with ten years' experience, this graduate should

be earning $10,000 per year. In 1959 there were a few places
where beginning salaries equalled or exceeded that $5,400
figure. Today, 1962, many agencies are paying that amount
for beginners with their master's degree, and some are top-
ping that, as the ads showed. Most social agencies have regular yearly raises (up to a limit), and there is rapid advancement for competent people. However, as of 1960, only 10 per
cent of social workers who had been in the field over ten years
were earning the $10,000 or more that the N.A.S.W. holds
as a desirable expectation.

A 1960 survey by the N.A.S.W. of its membership (mostly
professionally trained social workers) found that for the
2,400 social workers responding, the *average* salary was
$7,350 per year. (Average, in case you've forgotten statisti-
cal terms, means that all reported salaries were added together and then divided by the 2,400 salary earners.) The
median salary was $7,000 per year (which means that there
were as many responding N.A.S.W. social workers earning
over $7,000 per year as there were those earning *under* that
amount).

Salaries not only vary by the type of employing agency
but are higher or lower in different parts of the country.
Sometimes they are lower where actual costs of living are
lower. Sometimes they are lower where living costs are high,
but where climate and scenic beauties or cultural advantages
make up for less money. The struggle to get agency boards
and Community Chests and legislative bodies to pay adequately for the social workers they want will be a continu-
ing one, but there have been remarkable results in the last
few years. The steady rise of social work salaries reflects the

recognition by communities not only of the *need* for social work but of its value.

As you might expect, social agencies have developed socially advanced employment and personnel policies. Vacation arrangements are generous—usually four weeks with full salary. Sick leave allowances, insurance and pension plans are usually sound and good. Social workers are encouraged to take time for on-going study, to take special courses related to the advancement of their professional skills. Both time and money grants are given for attendance at national conferences on social welfare or social work problems.

The sharing of experiences between you and your colleagues, the continuous challenge to learn and understand more and better, and the learning experiences that good agencies provide through supervisory social workers and consultants from psychiatry, medicine, law, and other professions—all these are intangible but meaningful benefits to one whose interest in his work is keen and whose motivation to be helpful is high.

For Men Only: Men are entering social work in increasing numbers. It is our impression at the University of Chicago—probably borne out in other schools, too—that with the rumblings of nuclear war and destruction all about us, more young men want to throw their working efforts and energies into helping people, whether on a small or large scale. A 1960 study by the United States Bureau of Labor Statistics found that almost half (41%) of today's social work jobs are held by men. This is an interesting figure and trend because social work for so many years has been thought of as predominantly a woman's profession.

Let's be honest: it's a man's world, even in social work! Given equal competence a man is more likely to be promoted or chosen for executive, administrative, and public relations jobs than his female counterpart. (Mostly, however, the women seem to want it that way!) It is a fact that advancement for competent young men in social work is very rapid, and that men's salaries usually top those of women in equal positions. Partly this is because men are assumed to be responsible for providing for a family—or to be preparing for such responsibility. Partly it's because men have been in great demand and in scarcer supply.

Men are much needed in these areas: work with adolescent boys, (casework and group work), especially in the expanding work with street gangs and delinquents; work with boy and men probationers and parolees from prisons or reform schools; work within medical and psychiatric teams with male alcoholics, drug addicts, and the mentally ill who need emotional and social rehabilitation; work with husbands and fathers in marriage and parent-child problems. This is not to say that a man social worker deals only with men and boys. Far from it. It is only to say that these are *special* jobs where men are particularly valued.

Men are especially valued, too, for administrative and executive jobs that involve working with groups of men in other professions or in business. The major community organization jobs are carried by men, and increasingly men are being sought to head social agencies and special social work projects.

In short, the field of social work is cordial and open and

eager to use all the talents of capable young men and to offer them many opportunities.

For Women Only: If you've read the preceding section, you may be feeling wounded that *again* men and boys seem to have the edge on women in our society. But cheer up—there's still lots of room at the top in social work for the woman who chooses it as her career! And, moreover, it offers some very special benefits to women.

We assume in social work that a young woman looks forward to marriage and motherhood as part of her natural development as a woman. Not everyone achieves these roles, for lots of reasons—and if one remains unmarried, or is divorced or widowed, or is married and childless, the advantages of having a profession to pursue are clear to be seen. But what if you *do* get married and have a family—is there any point in going through the rigors and expense of professional preparation for social work? The answer seems to be an enthusiastic "Yes!" to judge by the reactions of many young and middle-aged married women in social work today.

First of all, education for social work is by its nature education for living in good relationships with other people. What you will learn in social work courses and field experience about the dynamics of the human personality and behavior, about the ways people create and can be helped to solve their problems—these will cast many new lights on your own behavior and on the ways in which wifehood and motherhood can be sustained and developed as happy and healthy experiences. Many of the young women who marry right after college and who, as they say, plan to "work my husband's way" through his prolonged schooling or until his

job yields better salary, attest to the personal values schooling in social work has had for them. But this is only "by
the way."

Many young women today, though married, continue to
work. Sometimes it's for financial reasons. In social work it's
often for reasons of the "pull" in the work: it's vital, it's important, it's interesting. (Secret: It makes even more interesting conversation with your husband than what you said to
the butcher when he tried to overcharge you!)

When babies come, you may want to leave work and give
yourself over fully to being a mother. This is good. But the
day may come—after your children go off to school, perhaps
—when you will want to reach out for refreshment and intellectual stimulation. If so, you may be able to find part-
time work in a social agency. Increasingly today social agencies are hiring professionally trained and experienced married women for limited hours or days per week.

When you reach middle age (if you can think that far
ahead) and your children go away to school or to live elsewhere, you can, with a refresher course or two, return to your
career. The common plaint of the middle-aged mother today
is that she has nothing to do with herself, "now that the children no longer need me." Often she casts about frantically
and futilely to find some interest or function for herself. The
woman who has a profession, even though she may have re-
tired from it temporarily, has something to go back to—she
has a future.

There are many jobs in social work where women are especially valued: work with adolescent girls, unhappy or delinquent; with little children who need "mothering persons";

with unmarried mothers and with adoptive parents; with groups of girls trying to develop social and occupational competences; with mothers of problem children and wives in unhappy marriages. Again, this is not to say that a woman social worker deals only with children and female clients. She has many men clients, too. And she often works in collaboration with men colleagues of her own or of other professions (doctors and psychiatrists, for example). But there are some special kinds of human wants where the mothering capacities of a woman are most useful and much valued.

For women social work offers a career that can, with some managing, be combined with careers as wife and mother; offers work that is useful, alive, challenging, and that enriches your personal life, too.

Why be a social worker? Chiefly because social work is more than a job. Its material rewards are modest, to be sure, and its frustrations are many. But its personal, intellectual, "inner-growth" rewards are rich. You will be in the mainstream of the life of man, in the hurly-burly of everyday living and its problems. You will be using yourself—your knowledge, and your personality—as an instrument of help to needful and often hurt people. You will be challenged to lift your eyes from what you do every day to envision and plan what might be done to bring about a better society.

That deeply human scientist, Albert Einstein, once wrote:

Strange is our situation here upon earth. Each of us comes for a short visit, not knowing why, yet sometimes seeming to divine a purpose. From the standpoint of daily life, however, there is one thing we know: That Man is here for the sake of other Men. . . . Above all, for those upon whose smile and well-being our own happiness depends, and also for the countless unknown souls with whose fate we are connected by a bond of sympathy. Many times a day I realize how much my own outer and inner life is built upon the labors of my fellow men, both living and dead, and how earnestly I must exert myself in order to give in return as much as I have received.

If you respond to this, if wholeheartedly you feel like saying, "Yes! I believe that, too!"—then the profession of social work is for you.

As I write these lines, there are to be heard all about us ominous rumblings of rockets and fall-out and exploits into outer space. And it occurs to me that social workers are among those few groups left who stubbornly affirm the importance of *inner* space. They are intent upon understanding the inner space of each man and on helping to build bridges between his mind and his heart and his actions. They are intent upon understanding the inner space of family life and helping to build stronger linkages among family members and between families and their fellow men. They are intent upon understanding the inner space of groups and communities and upon building two-way channels between man and the bewildering society of which he is part and purpose.

Perhaps in the final analysis these problems of inner space are what must interest you if you want to be a social worker. You and your fellow social workers may never be fully successful in solving them, but you will be the more human for having taken on the struggle!

SEVEN

Where to Find Out More

THIS CHAPTER is devoted to telling you just where you can get further information about prerequisite courses to prepare you for a school of social work, about the schools themselves, about social work jobs, or other questions you may have about social work in general.

Probably the most complete bibliography of materials available on all fields of social work has been published by the National Social Welfare Assembly, 345 East 46th Street, New York 17, New York. It is called *Social Work as a Career* and costs 25 cents. Actually, it was compiled for vocational and student counselors rather than for students themselves, but you may be interested in having a copy. Remember, it does not tell about social work; it is only a listing of available pamphlets and bulletins.

The two most useful information sources are the Council of Social Work Education, also located at 345 East 46th Street, New York City, and the National Association of Social Workers, 95 Madison Avenue, New York 16, New York. To save space and avoid repetition I will refer to the former as the C.S.W.E. and to the latter as the N.A.S.W. For Canadians: The Canadian Association of Social Workers has its office at 18 Rideau Street, Ottawa, Ontario.

About Social Work as a Career Choice

The C.S.W.E. has put together a Student Career Kit (#2) which will be sent to you for 50 cents. It contains a pamphlet describing the profession, leaflets about its various fields of practice issued by a number of national social work agencies, educational requirements for these fields, and so on. It is basic reading for many of your questions.

About Undergraduate College Courses

A number of colleges give courses about the field of social work or social welfare as part of their sociology or social psychology sequences. The C.S.W.E. will send you, on request, a list of undergraduate departments of colleges and universities that offer such courses.

In no sense are these courses held to be prerequisites for entry to a school of social work. Their best purpose probably is to give you some general ideas of the social work field and methods, and background for one of the jobs in social work that does not require professional training.

About Prerequisites for Entry to a School of Social Work

If you're not sure that the courses you're taking or planning to take in college will meet requirements of a school of social work, send for the catalogues of the two or three schools of social work that might be your preferred schools.

You'll find only very slight variations in what these schools suggest as necessary prerequisites. For a list of accredited schools of social work see below.

About Choice of Graduate School of Social Work

The names and locations of the sixty-three accredited schools of social work in the United States (including Hawaii and Puerto Rico) and Canada, as of July 1961, follow.

If you have any questions about a school that does not appear on this list, write to the C.S.W.E.

UNITED STATES

California

University of California, School of Social Welfare, Berkeley 4, California. Milton Chernin, Dean.

University of California at Los Angeles, School of Social Welfare, Los Angeles 24, California. Mary E. Duren, Acting Dean.

University of Southern California, School of Social Work, Los Angeles 7, California. Malcolm Stinson, Dean.

Colorado

University of Denver, School of Social Work, Denver 10, Colorado. Emil M. Sunley, Director.

Connecticut

University of Connecticut, School of Social Work, 1380 Asylum Avenue, Hartford 5, Connecticut. Harleigh B. Trecker, Dean.

District of Columbia

Catholic University of America, National Catholic School of Social Service, Washington 17, D.C. Frederick J. Ferris, Dean.

Howard University, School of Social Work, Washington 1, D.C. Mrs. Inabel Burns Lindsay, Dean.

Florida

Florida State University, School of Social Welfare, Graduate Program in Social Work, Tallahassee, Florida. Coyle E. Moore, Dean.

Georgia

Atlanta University School of Social Work, Atlanta, Georgia. William S. Jackson, Dean.

Hawaii

University of Hawaii, School of Social Work, Honolulu 14, Hawaii. Mrs. Katharine N. Handley, Director.

Illinois

University of Chicago, School of Social Service Administration, Chicago 37, Illinois. Alton A. Linford, Dean.

University of Illinois, School of Social Work, Urbana, Illinois. Mark Hale, Director.

Loyola University, School of Social Work, 820 North Michigan Avenue, Chicago 11, Illinois. Matthew H. Schoenbaum, Dean.

Indiana

Indiana University, Division of Social Service, 122 East Michigan Street, Indianapolis 4, Indiana. Mary Houk, Director.

Iowa

State University of Iowa, School of Social Work, Iowa City, Iowa. Frank Glick, Director.

Kansas

University of Kansas, Graduate Department of Social Work, Kansas City, Kansas. Joseph Meisels, Chairman.

Kentucky

University of Louisville, The Raymond A. Kent School of Social Work, Louisville 8, Kentucky. Arleigh L. Lincoln, Dean.

Louisiana

Louisiana State University, School of Social Welfare, Baton Rouge 3, Louisiana. Earl E. Klein, Director.

Tulane University, School of Social Work, New Orleans 18, Louisiana. Walter L. Kindelsperger, Dean.

Massachusetts

Boston College, School of Social Work, 126 Newbury Street, Boston 16, Massachusetts. The Rev. John V. Driscoll, S.J., Dean.

Boston University, School of Social Work, 264 Bay State Road, Boston 15, Massachusetts. John D. McDowell, Dean.

Simmons College, School of Social Work, 51 Commonwealth Avenue, Boston 16, Massachusetts. Robert F. Rutherford, Director.

Smith College School for Social Work, Northampton, Massachusetts. Howard J. Parad, Director.

Michigan

Michigan State University (College of Business and Public Service), School of Social Work, East Lansing, Michigan. Gordon J. Aldridge, Director.

University of Michigan, School of Social Work, Ann Arbor, Michigan. Fedele F. Fauri, Dean.

Wayne State University, School of Social Work, Detroit 2, Michigan. Charles B. Brink, Dean.

Minnesota

University of Minnesota, School of Social Work, Minneapolis 14, Minnesota. John C. Kidneigh, Director.

Missouri

University of Missouri, School of Social Work, Columbia, Missouri. Arthur W. Nebel, Director.

Saint Louis University, School of Social Service, 3801 West Pine Boulevard, St. Louis 3, Missouri. The Reverend A. H. Scheller, S.J., Director.

Washington University, The George Warren Brown School of Social Work, St. Louis 5, Missouri. Benjamin E. Youngdahl, Dean.

Nebraska

University of Nebraska, Graduate School of Social Work, Lincoln 8, Nebraska. Richard Guilford, Director.

New Jersey

Rutgers University, Graduate School of Social Work, New Brunswick, New Jersey. Wayne Vasey, Dean.

New York

Adelphi College, School of Social Work, Garden City, Long Island, New York. Arthur Katz, Dean.

University of Buffalo, School of Social Work, Buffalo 14, New York. Benjamin H. Lyndon, Dean.

Fordham University, School of Social Service, 134 East 39th Street, New York 16, New York. James W. Fogarty, Dean.

Hunter College, The Louis M. Rabinowitz School of Social Work, 695 Park Avenue, New York 21, New York. Paul Schreiber, Director.

New York School of Social Work of Columbia University, 2 East 91st Street, New York 28, New York. P. Fred Delli Quadri, Dean.

New York University, Graduate School of Social Work, Washington Square, New York 3, New York. Alex Rosen, Dean.

Syracuse University, School of Social Work, 400 Comstock Avenue, Syracuse 10, New York. Howard B. Gundy, Director.

Yeshiva University, School of Social Work, 110 West 57th St., New York 19, New York. Morton I. Teicher, Dean.

North Carolina

University of North Carolina, School of Social Work, Chapel Hill, North Carolina. Arthur E. Fink, Dean.

Ohio

Ohio State University, School of Social Work, Graduate Program, Columbus 10, Ohio. Everett C. Shimp, Director.

Western Reserve University, School of Applied Social Sciences, Cleveland 6, Ohio. Nathan E. Cohen, Dean.

Oklahoma

University of Oklahoma, School of Social Work, Norman, Oklahoma. C. Stanley Clifton, Director.

Pennsylvania

Bryn Mawr College, Carola Woerishoffer Graduate Department of Social Work and Social Research, Bryn Mawr, Pennsylvania. Mrs. Katherine D. Lower, Director.

University of Pennsylvania, School of Social Work, 2410 Pine Street, Philadelphia 3, Pennsylvania. Ruth E. Smalley, Dean.

University of Pittsburgh, Graduate School of Social Work, Pittsburgh 13, Pennsylvania. Wilber I. Newstetter, Dean.

Puerto Rico

University of Puerto Rico, School of Social Work, Rio Piedras, Puerto Rico. Georgina Pastor, Director.

Tennessee

University of Tennessee, School of Social Work, 810 Broadway, Nashville 3, Tennessee. Sue Spencer, Director.

Texas

Our Lady of the Lake College, Worden School of Social Service, San Antonio 7, Texas. Sister Mary Immaculate, Director.

University of Texas, School of Social Work, Austin 12, Texas. Lora Lee Pederson, Director.

Utah

University of Utah, Graduate School of Social Work, Salt Lake City 1, Utah. Rex A. Skidmore, Dean.

Virginia

College of William and Mary, School of Social Work, Richmond Professional Institute, 800 West Franklin Street, Richmond 20, Virginia. George T. Kalif, Director.

Washington

University of Washington, School of Social Work, Seattle 5, Washington. Victor I. Howery, Dean.

West Virginia

West Virginia University, Department of Social Work, Morgantown, West Virginia. Bernhard Scher, Chairman.

Wisconsin

University of Wisconsin, School of Social Work, Madison 6, Wisconsin. Ersel E. Le Masters, Director.

CANADA

British Columbia

University of British Columbia, School of Social Work, Vancouver 8, British Columbia. William G. Dixon, Director.

Manitoba

University of Manitoba, School of Social Work, Winnipeg, Manitoba. Helen Mann, Director.

Ontario

University of Ottawa, St. Patrick's College School of Social Welfare, Ottawa, Ontario. The Reverend Swithun Bowers, O.M.I., Director.
University of Toronto, School of Social Work, Toronto 5, Ontario. Charles E. Hendry, Director.

Quebec

Laval University, School of Social Work, Quebec, Quebec. Simone Paré, Director.

McGill University, School of Social Work, 3600 University Street, Montreal 2, Quebec. John J. O. Moore, Director. Université de Montréal, L'Ecole de Service Social, C. P. 6128, Montreal, Quebec. Rev. Andre-M. Guillemette, O.P., Director.

Write directly to the dean or the director of the schools you're interested in, asking for a catalogue. In it you will find something about the school's history, its objectives, its faculty, what it considers to be its special strengths and interests, its explicit statement of the courses offered, its tuition and living cost figures, its available scholarship grants, and so forth.

Remember that the early application (preferably in the fall of your senior year at college) gets early consideration and decision. It leaves you time, too, to turn elsewhere if your first choice turns you down.

About Scholarships and Money Aid

Every two years the C.S.W.E. publishes a compilation, *Social Work Fellowships and Scholarships in the United States and Canada.* The current one is for 1961-1963. Price $1.00.

As indicated above, the catalogue of every school of social work contains information on its particular tuition and scholarship aids.

About Jobs

Part-time or try-out jobs during Summer Vacations, Volunteer or Paid

The Y.M.C.A.'s, Y.W.C.A.'s, Scout organizations and often settlement houses, community centers, or neighborhood houses use college men and women as group leaders for children and adolescents. Summer camps under the auspices of such social agencies take on counselors or recreation aides.

Your community Council of Social Agencies or Welfare Council or United Community Fund (find out what the particular name is in your community) may have a Careers for Social Work program. These are summer job opportunities set up in family and child welfare agencies—and sometimes in hospital and clinic settings, too—for college students who are interested in becoming social workers. Eight cities (all east of St. Louis) now have such programs, but the social agencies in a number of other cities all over the country are working on developing such plans.

Even if there is no Careers for Social Work program in your city or town, some of the agencies may have summer openings of a clerical, receptionist, or case aide (helper to a caseworker) sort. Most agencies would prefer more rather than less mature people—so your chances are better if you're twenty-ish and well into college.

The Department of Public Welfare (aid to families, old people, and children) may take on a part-time, fill-in case aide now and then. (See below.)

Large psychiatric hospitals or hospitals and schools for mentally deficient or nerve-damaged children often need and want to hire summer casework aides. Usually these institutions are in rural settings, requiring that you drive a car or perhaps live in. Again, your Council of Social Agencies or its equivalent ought to be able to tell you who the medical or social service director is to whom you can write.

Full-time Jobs as a Social Worker without Professional Education

When you are a college graduate, three kinds of jobs are open to you without professional social work training:

a) In public assistance agencies as a caseworker (often called investigator, home visitor, case aide) where you would carry cases of families and single persons whose primary need is for financial assistance. Call or write your city, county or state Department of Public Welfare (sometimes listed as Public Aid or Public Assistance) for information about openings and requirements.

b) In recreational agencies as group worker or group work aide. Agencies most interested in college graduates for staff positions are "Y's" (YMCA and YMHA), Scouts, settlement and community centers that have boys' and girls' clubs and recreation activities. Phone calls to such agencies in any community will tell you if there are vacancies. If you are interested in work as a recreation leader in another part of the country, you may write for possible information about openings to one of the following major national group work and recreation agencies.

American National Red Cross, 17th and D Streets NW, Washington 13, D.C.

Boy Scouts of America, New Brunswick, New Jersey

Boys' Clubs of America, 771 First Avenue, New York 17, New York

Camp Fire Girls, 16 East 48th Street,
New York 17, New York

Girl Scouts of the U.S.A., 830 Third Avenue,
New York 22, New York

National Board of the Y.W.C.A., 600 Lexington Avenue,
New York 22, New York

National Federation of Settlements and Neighborhood
Centers, 226 West 47th Street, New York 36, New York

National Jewish Welfare Board, 145 East 32nd Street,
New York 16, New York

Young Men's Christian Associates of the United States of
America, National Council, 291 Broadway, New York 7,
New York

c) In correctional work. Courts, especially those dealing
with problems of delinquent youth, are increasingly concerned to get adequate probation and parole workers. These
are demanding and difficult jobs; actually they call for wide
knowledge and high skill. But there is far more need than
there are trained workers, so there are openings for college
graduates in beginning positions. The names and addresses
of the probation and parole departments in your community
can be had from the National Council on Crime and Delinquency, 44 East 23 Street, New York 10, New York.

Full-time Jobs Requiring Professional Education

If you're curious about what kinds of position are open
to trained social workers (beyond the samples you've seen

in Chapter 6), write to the N.A.S.W. and ask that they send you an issue of *Personnel Information*. This is a listing of openings for caseworkers, group workers, community workers, executives, supervisors, researchers, in every state of the Union. It is sent out bimonthly to N.A.S.W. members, and a sample copy will be sent you on request. (There are other places where ads for social workers are published, too—in the journal, *Social Casework*, for instance, and in the bulletin of the Social Work Vocational Bureau, but *Personnel Information* is the easiest to get.)

About Social Work in General

There is one reference book that may be found in almost every public or college library. (If your library doesn't have it, tell the librarian about it!) It is the *Social Work Year Book* (latest edition 1960, but earlier editions hold much that is still useful), published by N.A.S.W.; cost, $8.50. This volume contains articles describing all fields of social work practice; social work's history, trends, activities; discussion of the major problems and solutions in social work's planning and operations; selected bibliographies on each subject for your further information; a complete directory of national and international social agencies and their functions. It is, in short, a little gold mine of social work information and will provide answers to many of your questions or lead you to where the answers may be found.

The N.A.S.W. is the major source of information on social work's personnel practices, ethics, salaries, and professional problems and practices. Your written inquiry will bring a helpful response. (Responses are better when you say exactly what it is you want to know, rather than "please send me everything you have on social work." The latter floors the respondent, and it might floor you, too, if he sent everything he had!)

If you'd like to talk directly to someone who is in social work and who knows it well, two suggestions:

a) A request to the N.A.S.W. will bring you the name and address of the chairman of the local chapter nearest to where you live. If the chairman can't arrange to see you, he'll see that someone else representing the chapter will.

b) If you are near a school of social work, a letter or phone call asking for an appointment to talk about your interest in a social work career will bring you an appointment with one of the faculty.

What you will find, wherever you turn, is that the profession of social work is keenly aware of the growing need for trained social workers, and through its national and local agencies it is involved in many recruitment efforts. Social workers and social agencies are glad to answer your inquiries and questions about social work. If you have the necessary qualifications to enter graduate education for social work, or if you are still at the stage of trying to decide whether social work is or is not the career for you, you will find that its practitioners will be ready and glad to help you by answering your questions or telling you what you want to know, either in person or by the many printed interpretations that are yours for the asking. If you qualify—you are welcome!

INDEX

ABOUT THE AUTHOR

I fell into social work. When I graduated from college, at the University of Minnesota, I was bent on being a newspaper woman, (specialty human-interest stories) or an advertising copy-writer (specialty, giving glamorous names to perfumes). But I needed money while I looked for these heady jobs, so I asked for, and—to my amazement—got, a job as a temporary caseworker in a family welfare agency. When, at the summer's end, the advertising job came along I was too deep in the poignant details of my clients' lives to be able to leave them.

Several years later, as I became increasingly intrigued and mystified by the complexities of human beings and their life cycles, I undertook graduate study in social work. I got my M. S. degree at the New York School of Social Work, Columbia University.

Family casework (particularly marital and parent-child problems) child guidance and school social work have been my fields of practice and supervisory concentration. I have been on the faculty of the University of Chicago's School of Social Service Administration for a number of years, professor of social work since 1959. I am married and have a son.

Teaching and being a wife and a mother are my favorite occupations. I love to travel—but, then, who doesn't? When

I sit down I like to read, or have a good talk, or play a mean game of scrabble. I write for fun sometimes, and I've had a few short stories and poems published. Mostly I write for professional journals. My book, *Social Casework—A Problem Solving Process* (1957), is in its sixth printing and has, to date, been translated into Dutch, Japanese, and Swedish.